WHEN
I MET
Jesus

A LIFELONG JOURNEY
OF FAITH, HOPE AND TRUST

DEBRA MOORE EWING

WHEN I MET JESUS
A Lifelong Journey of Faith, Hope and Trust

ISBN: 979-8-9857622-0-4

Cover and Interior Design
by Transcendent Publishing
www.transcendentpublishing.com

Printed in the United States of America.

Author's note: Some names and identifying details have been changed to protect the confidentiality of those involved. When actual names were used, I was granted their permission.

www.ingramcontent.com/pod-product-compliance
Lightning Source LLC
Chambersburg PA
CBHW060514130626
46553CB00002B/498

MY MISSION

*To comfort those who are grieving
or nearing transition, and replace fear with faith
by sharing my visits with Jesus.*

ACKNOWLEDGMENTS

To my teachers, past, present, and across the veil, thank you for giving me the courage and safe haven to follow your guidance, soak in your knowledge and pay it forward to be a lighthouse for others. I also owe a debt of gratitude to Tom Bird's Writing Retreats for teaching me how to "open the door."

Special thanks to my mother, my best friend, who always supported and believed in me even when she didn't understand.

I so appreciate my friend and publisher, Shanda Trofe. Thank you for guiding me through the publishing process!

And to my hubby, Bill, for bringing breakfast, lunch, and dinner to me as I was writing. Your support and respect for my writing time behind the closed doors of our shared office space was appreciated more than you know!

… and to Jesus. I can't put words to the feeling I hold dear in the depths of my being. I look forward to our future conversations. Thank You. I have now learned to Trust the Process!

I am grateful for the gifts you gave me. I love you all!

TABLE OF CONTENTS

INTRODUCTION

It was close to midnight. The room of the bunkhouse I shared with several other teenaged girls was dark and quiet. Everyone else was sleeping peacefully, worn out from a day of sun and fresh air at summer camp, but I lay there, wide awake, the thoughts running through my mind like the proverbial hamster on a wheel. Then my stomach started to churn with nausea as the guilt consumed every fiber of my being. What had I done? My heart started racing, and I could feel it through the lightly draped sheet that covered me. Finally, after trying, unsuccessfully, to rationalize everything, at least enough to drift off to sleep, I began to pray.

Sleeping on the top bunk gave me a clear view of the small square window that looked out over the water of the breathtaking Princess Louisa Inlet on the coast of British Columbia. As I tossed and turned, finally ending up on my back, I saw moonlight peering through the window where it danced back and forth across the ceiling. I took in a deep breath and caught the faint smell of the saltwater close by. In the distance I could hear the comforting sound of waves lapping against the shore.

As I continued praying to God, I noticed a shadow off to my left at the foot of the bed. Curious, I sat up, wanting to make sure it wasn't my imagination. Then the shadow seemed to shift, or possibly it was the movement of the moon, because there, standing at the left corner of my bunk, was a person. Startled, my first thought was that someone must have snuck into our cabin.

What happened next was inconceivable and, I think you will agree, unexplainable as well. Perhaps this is why I have kept the story deep inside for fifty-two years. Now, as I find myself in the last third of my life, I knew I couldn't waste any more time; I knew it was something He wants you to hear.

I realize that in writing this I am possibly opening myself up to the armchair critics, but that's okay. My goal is to trust the process and hopefully fill your hearts with love, erase fear and give you a sense of renewed faith and hope so you can fully live and enjoy your life. Having faith isn't difficult. At least for me it wasn't, and that is why I need to share my story. I want you to *feel* what I do.

Do you believe in God, have faith in the unknown, and have confidence in the written word? It's sometimes challenging to have faith when life throws you a curve ball you didn't see coming. There are times it isn't easy to keep going.

If you have lost a loved one or a child, it must be unbearable to move past the grief. If you recently lost your job, are going through a break-up or divorce, or like me, received a life-altering health diagnosis, fear of the unknown may consume you. I honestly get it! Having faith is hard. It is easy for me to tell you to have faith, but why would you believe me unless you know the challenges I have faced in life or what and who I have seen?

In the 1980s I started writing a book to help women gain confidence and feel more empowered in their lives. Like myself, so many young girls were brought up with promises by their mothers that they would get married, raise a family, and have the white picket fence. The movie Cinderella didn't help either! Indeed, one of my favorite assumptions about how life "should" be was that my prince charming would show up and sweep me off my feet.

When that didn't happen, it was natural to wonder what was wrong with me. It is hard enough to see a thirty-year-old woman grovel at the crumbs a man would throw her way, but I find it devastating to see a woman in her fifties who is still struggling, especially since I know I can help them. That is the book I was supposed to finish, but God had different ideas, and thankfully I was listening. I believe the COVID-19 pandemic had something to do with it. Quarantined in your own home and unable to be around people, you can only watch so much television or read. So I spent a lot of quality time quietly, by myself, enjoying the silence. And that's when I heard Him telling me it was time. I had always heard that everyone has a book inside them, and that if you find the time to get quiet and go within, the words will come – and now I know that's true.

As I think about my story and how I will ever begin to share it, I have a question for you. What if I told you that when I was fifteen, I physically saw Jesus? Would you believe me? Or would you think I was smoking something, or at the very least making the story up? And, even crazier, what if I told you Jesus came to me at three-thirty-one morning in early 2021 and said, *Write the book, finish it and give it away for free.*

I remember thinking, *That was interesting,* before falling back asleep. In the morning, when I reflected on the experience I realized it was quite different from His previous visits, because this time we had a complete, two-way conversation. I remembered telling Him that nobody would believe me. He told me to trust the process, and that became my mantra. He said, *It only takes one, and that person will share, and another, and so on.*

You can imagine my surprise that when I did sit down to start writing the book, I was not the only one writing it! Yes, this story is one I have a burning desire to share, but *He* came through my fingertips on the keyboard faster than I even knew I could type! The words just flew, and I had to stop in between to shake out my hands and fingers so I could continue!

Jesus has told me time and time again that trust is the key. Well, I am trusting the process, and I am trusting Him. I hope you will read along and trust it too, because there are things He wants you to know.

CHAPTER ONE

EARLY YEARS

After seven years of trying, my mother was shocked and happy to learn that she was finally pregnant with me. As I write this, I am laughing. *Be careful what you wish for, Mom!*

I was born in 1954 in Washington State, where we lived in a one-stoplight town called Redmond. Mom always said we lived in a double garage, and that irritated me. Maybe it started out that way, but, thanks to my father, who was a custom homebuilder, it had evolved into the one-bedroom home that my parents and I shared. Eventually, Dad purchased the adjacent property from my uncle and built a larger home in front of the "little house," as my parents now called it.

When I was three years old, my mother gave birth to a boy, Jim. From the start, I thought my little brother was the best thing that ever happened. I remember running my fingers over the silky-soft skin of his arm, and watching, fascinated, that he was able to rub the binding on his blanket against the bridge of his nose while simultaneously sucking his two fingers.

We have so many beautiful memories from our childhood. There was a big pasture out front where in the early days my grandfather kept pigs, chickens, beef cattle, and sheep. I remember the sheep mostly, especially the tiny black one, which was my favorite. Looking back, I realize it's because I was aware that I too was different from those around me, that little black lamb was a metaphor for my life.

My grandfather also had a garden with rows of boysenberry bushes as big as my daddy's thumb. They were so delicious, freshly picked, and in the pies Grandma baked, with a crumble of butter, sugar, and flour on top. She also made pies with the rhubarb grown by my grandfather, but those were too tart for my taste. Mostly, I loved when Grandma taught me how to bake, cookies as well as pies. Snickerdoodles were my favorite, and she always let me lick the beaters. Every August 13, my brother Jim and I would go to Grandma's to bake and decorate a cake for our parents' wedding anniversary. Jimmie and I would fight over who got to eat the icing or the corner of the cake, but we each always got a beater. One of my fondest memories, though, is when Grandma made her pineapple upside-down cake. When she passed, that plate was the one possession of hers that I wanted – well, that and her aprons, of course.

There was a huge towering maple tree in the pasture. The leaves would change to beautiful hues of yellow and orange near the approach of fall. Nestled underneath its branches was a rope swing and giant boulders, where Jimmie and I spent countless hours making forts and playing with the neighbor kids. Cake icing aside, my brother and I always got along and had fun. Looking back on those days, I feel sorry for the children growing up today, many of whom don't get the chance to experience something like that. There are condominiums and apartments and cookie-cutter housing developments that typically don't have a giant space to run and play. Electronics, cell phones, video games, and the like have replaced fresh air and childhood creativity. My brother and I often played cowboys and Indians, which is not politically correct these days but was, if I'm being honest, great fun. Other times we would run from our home down to the tree, yelling at the top of our lungs the line from our favorite cartoon – "Here I come to save the day! Mighty Mouse is on his way!" – in the hopes that Terry and Chris, who lived next door, would hear us and run over to play.

When our parents announced that my mother was pregnant, we were so excited. It was 1963 and I was in the fourth grade, old enough to think about all the ways I could help with a new baby. I wondered if it would be a girl, while I'm sure Jimmie was hoping for a little brother he could play with in the pasture.

We were raised in the Lutheran faith. Mom and Dad went to church every Sunday, and Jimmie and I attended Sunday school. I didn't like going to church as a child. I never enjoyed sitting in the pews and pretending to listen to the minister when I would rather be outside playing or watching cartoons, but Sunday School was fun. That is where we learned about God. I also remember enjoying crafts, cutting shapes out of construction paper, and gluing them to create a pretty project to bring home.

It was the first week of June 1964 when the baby decided to come. Our grandparents came to take care of us while our parents went to the hospital. You can only imagine the excitement and enthusiasm we all had. I prayed every single night to God, asking Him for the baby to be okay. Later, it would strike me as odd that I prayed for something like this. Why wouldn't I ask God to bring me a sister, like most kids my age? And, it was only much later, after discovering my gifts, that this was possibly one of my early precognitive visions.

Steven Duncan Moore was born on June 3, 1964, and sadly passed eighteen hours later. Our world immediately fell apart. I never told anyone that I thought it was my fault. Jimmie and I were not told how Steven died, only that it was a blood condition. In my ten-year-old mind, I thought God must have felt I was selfish by asking someone as powerful as Him to make sure my baby brother or sister was okay. I even thought Steven's death was punishment for something I had possibly done. I never told my mom I felt this way, and as an adult I came to realize it was ridiculous; back then, however, and for years afterward, the guilt weighed heavily on me.

To make matters worse, we quit going to church. I remember hearing my mom say through her tears, "Why would God do this?" She was not only hurt, but mad. A couple of months later, my parents purchased a christening bowl stand in Steven's memory, but I do not remember returning to Sunday school. That was it. God had taken my baby brother, and we were done with Him.

My parents had a tough time that year, especially Mom. Years later, when I found out she hadn't cared whether she lived or died, I asked, "Even though you had Jimmie and me?" and she replied, "Yes." I didn't fully understand the extent of her grief, however, until my husband and I went through it after I miscarried during my first pregnancy. Even though it was early on we were devastated, and I couldn't imagine how it must feel to carry a child to full-term and then lose it. Truthfully, I don't know if I would have wanted to live either.

Five years later, in August 1969, church came knocking on my door again – this time with a group of the kids I hung around. We attended Christian meetings together, and I found myself enjoying them as much as I had Sunday school.

Looking back, I'm surprised that my parents let me go to the camp in British Columbia. Though it was a beautiful place situated on the water with many activities and a great group of people, I was just fifteen, and my seventeen-year-old high school sweetheart, Tom, planned on going with me. Of course, in 1969 the world was completely different than it is today, when teenagers dating is cause for concern. The fact that the camp was Christian probably made them more comfortable as well.

Camp was even better than I thought it would be. There was water skiing, rowboats, swimming, golfing, crafts, contests, singing, and more.

Plus I got to meet kids from all over Canada and the States. It was truly an incredible week.

One day Tom and I decided to spend some time by ourselves exploring the area. We got a rowboat and paddled out to his little island. It was tiny, with a couple of trees and covered with moss. The water was so clear we could see there was an oyster bed surrounding us. Tom and I relaxed on this beautiful soft, lush emerald-green velvety bed, listening to the trickle of the waves and a few birds in the distance. We were enjoying every minute of basking in the sun, something we didn't see a lot of in Seattle! It was an incredibly intimate moment, and I was so much in love I believed we would be together forever. While it feels strange sharing something so deeply personal, it is essential to this story. I gave myself, all of me, to the young man with whom I thought would share my life.

I don't remember much of the day afterward; however, that evening, while lying in my bunk bed in the girls' cabin, I was wracked with guilt. My parents had raised me to wait for your wedding day before sharing such an intimate part of yourself. It is a gift from God, they said, and not something to be given away to just anybody, so you can imagine the feeling of condemnation that filled my soul. I felt tarnished, "used up," like a terrible person. Of course I couldn't undo it; nor could I erase those awful thoughts from my mind. I was so distraught that I felt physically nauseous, and with tears flowing down my cheeks I talked to God, silently so I wouldn't wake the other girls, begging Him for forgiveness. I knew what I had done was wrong. I had let Him down, and if my parents found out they would be deeply disappointed as well. I remember telling myself, "Debbie, it's okay. You and Tom will get married after high school. He loves you as much as you love him. It's okay." That did assuage the guilt somewhat, but it certainly didn't erase it, so I started to pray again.

At some point I opened my eyes and there, down by my feet, a beam of moonlight was streaming in through the small window – just enough so I could see the shadow standing off to the left. Thinking it was my imagination, I scooted down toward the end of the bed and was startled to find a man in a white robe with shoulder-length brown wavy hair, olive skin, and gentle eyes standing there. I blinked to make sure I wasn't dreaming, then I leaned over to reach out and touch Him with my right hand. As I did, He disappeared, but I had no doubt as to who it was. The man was Jesus! I looked around the room, hoping to see Him again, but He wasn't there. How could that be? How did that happen? It was what I imagine a ghost encounter to be like, but this was no ghost. It was real, and it was – and still is – the most fantastic thing that has ever happened to me!

Disappointed at not having touched Him, I moved back up toward the pillow and lay down. More than that, I was utterly amazed by what had just happened. But I never for a minute doubted that it was real. Jesus had heard me! He had listened to my prayers. Intuitively, I knew He had felt the pain in my heart and came to let me know He had forgiven me. Wow! This camp is something special, I thought. That would never have happened sitting in a church pew! Jesus' appearance had certainly made me feel better; now I wondered how I could share this incredible experience, or whether I should even do so. Would anyone even believe me?

CHAPTER TWO

HORMONAL TEENS

Jesus would come to visit several times throughout my troubled teenage years. I don't remember sharing my stories with anyone which, given what a blabbermouth I was, was unusual. I just couldn't help thinking others would think I was crazy or hallucinating. It was, after all, the sixties, and mescaline, speed, Black Beauties, LSD, and of course, sex, were readily abundant. It was the free love era, and sex – lots of it and with many partners – was considered an expression of the self. I had stayed away from drugs; I was too afraid of horrifying hallucinations and the possibility that they might cause birth defects to my future children. As for sex, well you saw how guilty I felt about that one time at camp!

So while many other kids were running wild, I, at fifteen, decided I wanted to model. I wanted to be like the glamourous, beautiful women I saw in magazines and on TV. I convinced my parents by pointing out how much time they devoted to my brother and his sports. Knowing Mom always wanted things to be *even* between us, I would tease her, saying, "You love Jimmie more than you love me," to which she always replied, "I love you both the same."

We found a modeling school in downtown Seattle where I not only learned how to model but was taught etiquette and social graces as well. It was my dream, but unfortunately, Twiggy was the icon we were all expected to emulate, and she was pencil-thin. The owners of the school were on some of us constantly to lose weight. I was five feet eight inches and weighed one hundred thirty-five pounds – way too much, they said. Looking back, I realize how ridiculous and harmful that was, and how lucky I am that I didn't develop anorexia or bulimia like so many other girls do. I did start taking diet pills, though, figuring that since the doctor had prescribed them to my parents they must be okay.

I still have some photographic slides of my modeling days, and when I look at them I can only shake my head in amazement. What on earth was wrong with me? I know I'm not alone in this, that there are many women who revisit photos of their younger days and wonder why they mentally beat themselves up about their appearance. Why did we do this? Why did we think we were fat? The answer is simple: we let society and unattainable standards keep us on a constant diet merry-go-round. After all, this was a time when stewardesses (flight attendants) had to weigh in, and if they were "overweight" they could lose their job! If we only knew then what we know now, life would have been so much easier!

One thing's for sure, I never felt like any of those beautiful models. I never thought I was thin enough, so I was never good enough either. It also didn't help that I entered beauty pageants. Nothing can destroy a young girl's self-esteem quicker than beauty pageants! I was always the runner-up or second or third place, and certainly I assumed my weight was partly the reason. Still trying to achieve the impossible dream, I spiraled out of control, taking diet pills, sometimes two a day. As they were essentially "uppers" I had difficulty sleeping at night, which affected my schoolwork.

As for my relationship with Tom, it did not turn out to be the "forever love" I'd hoped for. In fact, he wasn't the person I thought him to be.

After we broke up, the authorities caught up with him for some past offenses, and he would wind up spending the rest of his life in prison. I did remain good friends with his fraternal twin, Mick (we are still close today), and I've often wondered how two children raised by the same parents could turn out so differently.

In 1971, when I was sixteen, my dad bought me a candy apple red Mustang. It had chrome Cragar mags and dual exhaust; black sidewall tires with raised white lettering; and taillights similar to a California Special. I guess that is when my passion for vehicles got started, though it could also have been at the age of four, when I drove my dark green "Kidillac" pedal car on my parents' patio. As for the Mustang, I can remember everything down to the minute detail, but I think what I loved most was the noise it made when I started her up!

It was while in the Mustang that I was visited by Jesus for the second time. One night, I was driving home on the Bell-Red Road, which is the connector between Redmond and the city of Bellevue. The road curved sharply by the nursery at the top of our street, which was dangerous if someone wasn't familiar with it. Suddenly, a car headed in the opposite direction swerved over, crossing the center line into my lane! I immediately veered to the right and fortunately escaped what would have been a devastating head-on collision. Trembling and shaking at the near-miss, I saw in my peripheral vision a shadow in the passenger seat. I glanced over, and for a fleeting moment there was Jesus, sitting in the car with me! Though it was very brief, I know He came to let me know I was not alone. Of course, you don't understand these things at sixteen, and in my case there was no one I felt safe talking to about it, not even my parents. If I had, they probably would have thought I was on drugs.

Which brings me to my third visit. My father was an accomplished, award-winning builder, which afforded us a very comfortable life. Growing up, I didn't realize it. It was just how things were. The A-frame cabin, on fifty feet of waterfront on Lake Sammamish, was where we spent our summers. Boaters would stop daily to marvel at the cabin's unique design that had exposed bright orange beams. I was so proud of my dad; after all, I took after him. I had the building gene as well. Of all the gifts he gave me the one I was most excited about was a toolbox.

The home we grew up in was only about a mile away, so it was convenient to go back and forth if necessary. But as kids Jimmie and I loved staying at the cabin so we could wake up there and head right to the lake to swim or go skiing. I remember playing with my Barbie dolls in the sand when I was younger, and I loved looking for rocks. One time I found an arrowhead, and I enjoyed imagining the Native Americans being on our beach in earlier times.

When the neighbor next door announced he was selling his cabin and boathouse, my father decided to buy them. That gave us one hundred feet of waterfront, plus all the property behind on the hillside on which to build. Dad hired a very talented architect for his passion project, and the result was a two-story home nestled amongst the trees, with large decks on the front looking out onto the water. It was fantastic, and became a gathering place for my friends who came for barbeques, swimming, lounging on the beach and water skiing.

It was in that house that Jesus came to me again. My bedroom was on the lower northeast corner of the second story. I had a full bathroom, a separate area for my desk so I could study, and a nice-sized sleeping area with a door leading out to the deck. I don't remember much of what was transpiring in my life at the time, aside from another issue compounded by my abuse of the diet pills. One night, about a year after my close call in the Mustang, I was lying in bed with the nightstand lamp on when I suddenly saw Jesus standing by the door leading to the deck. He was not transparent and, like the other times, He vanished into thin air as quickly as He'd appeared. At the time I didn't realize the significance of the visit but, looking back, I feel as if He wanted me to know that He was there. Whatever the reason, it would be the last time I saw Him for many years.

CHAPTER THREE

EMBRACING MY UNIQUENESS

G rowing up, I knew that I was a little different from some of my friends, but I attributed it to, of all things, the fact that I was a Pisces. From what I read, Pisces, a water sign, can be more in tune with their intuition and things of a spiritual nature.

My mother had another explanation, that I must have gotten my spiritual side from Grandma Moore, my dad's mother. She too was a "little *different*," as Mom would say when trying to describe her personality.

Grandma Moore, or Nana, as she liked to be called, was very different from my other grandmother, who lived near us on Lake Sammamish. Nana, who became a widow at a young age, lived across the country in Philadelphia, where she worked in a drugstore. I will never forget visiting her as a child and being absolutely amazed by her apartment, which was decorated entirely in shades of pink, right down to the telephone, refrigerator and stove! I don't remember if she had a pink couch, but I'm sure she accented with pink pillows. And, unlike my other grandmother who had a fuller figure and wore Model Coats (you know, the kind that snapped up the front?) and house slippers, Nana was very slender and wore frilly blouses. She also didn't bake; in fact, I don't think she cooked much at all, but preferred to pick up things at the deli. While I loved

Nana, I didn't get to know her very well as she was afraid to fly and never came out to visit. I apparently took after her, though, and know for a fact that we shared at least one thing in common: we both loved to write poetry.

As mentioned, my maternal grandparents were constants in my life, and my grandfather, who passed in 1973, was the first major loss I endured. Of course, it was harder on my grandmother. Sixteen years his junior, she had spent her entire adult life with him, and I wondered how she would go on alone.

My grandfather and I were very close; I adored him, and he would do anything I asked. When I was in grade school, he allowed me to sit on his lap in his 1960s-era turquoise Ford pickup and drive down the Lake Sammamish Road to his and Grandma's home. I remember his friendly smile and his twinkly blue eyes as he sat patiently and let me style his hair with bobby pins. In the early years he smoked cigarettes, and I would watch, fascinated, as the smoke came swirling out with each exhale. Like most kids, I emulated the behavior of the adults around me, so I suppose it was inevitable that I would want to try it for myself. One week they stayed with me and Jimmie while our parents were on vacation, and I asked if I could see what it was like to smoke a cigarette. As I mentioned, my granddaddy would do *anything* for me, and before I knew it I was sneaking into my parents' bathroom at the back of the house so Grandma wouldn't find out, and so I could watch myself in the mirror to see if I looked cool. Thankfully, the disgusting taste, and the ensuing coughing fit, ended my curiosity.

Sometime in 1979, six years after my grandfather passed, he came to me. I was sleeping, but it was too real to be merely a dream. Aside from nightmares, most of my dreams were rather vague and forgotten by the time I woke up. This one, however, was extremely vivid, and remains so to this day.

In this dream, my granddad was wearing the blue and white pin-striped overalls that he wore when he was working. He was a truck driver for the Pioneer Fruit Company in Seattle and, I am proud to say, he was a Teamster. (I'm also sure that even in spirit, he appreciates that I followed in his footsteps and joined a union as well). He was at the beach, standing on the walkway that led to the floating dock on Lake Sammamish.

It was a sight I knew well from when he was alive. My grandparents had a twenty-five-foot lot next to ours with a small house nestled on the hill that my father had built for them before I was born. There was a trail leading from their steps to the beach, and at the end was their "boathouse." I don't know why they called it that because it had single beds inside – maybe because my uncle stored his small sailboat there during the winter. Like their main house, it too had a deck and then a couple of steps past my favorite tree, an enormous weeping willow. Whenever the wind picked up, the branches with their delicate leaves would blow and sway in the breeze. I always thought that tree was magnificent!

Granddad just stood there and smiled. The sun was glistening on his tanned skin, and the lake was sparkling in the sun's reflection. He looked to be in his early seventies and still robust, though he had been eighty-five and ill when he passed.

"I am okay, Debits," he said, using his special nickname for me. I don't remember seeing his lips move, so chances are he spoke telepathically. Afterward, I woke up hysterically sobbing, so loud it woke up my fiancé at the time, but I couldn't understand it, let alone explain what had happened. I had never experienced a dream like that, and I now understand that these are not dreams at all, but *visits* from spirit, as real as when I had seen Jesus.

Ultimately, my fiancé and I broke up. There were just too many red flags for me, and after seeing my best friend go through two divorces,

I believed I would never recover from something like that. It had to be right the first, and only, time.

Since I could not afford the apartment we lived in by myself, I moved in with my girlfriend Debbie and her eight-year-old son, Shane. She lived in the apartment complex across the street so it was convenient, plus I had never lived alone before and it was nice to have her support as I healed from the breakup.

It was there, at Debbie's house, that I had my first precognitive dream. Of course, I didn't know that at the time; I just thought it was a terrible nightmare. In the dream, Shane and his friends were playing with peashooters and he swallowed a straight pin. I immediately sat up in bed, horrified and sickened that I would dream of such an awful thing! And why a straight pin? Weren't they called "pea shooters" for a reason?

Eventually I fell back to sleep and when I woke the following morning the dream was long forgotten. A little while later, I was sitting on the couch in her living room having coffee when I heard the front door open and slam shut, then saw Shane scrambling up the stairs with lightning speed. Before I could even ask what happened Debbie and Shane came running back down the stairs. "I have to take Shane to the hospital," she cried, "He swallowed a straight pin!" As quickly as she said it, they were out the door.

I remember sitting on the couch in horror as memories of the dream I'd had just hours before returned and raced through my mind. How could I dream something so frightening about someone I loved? It had to have been my fault, I thought. I had dreamed it, and that is why it happened! For quite some time I sat there, so sick inside I thought I might vomit.

When Debbie and Shane came home she told me the pin had showed up on the X-ray, and now they just had to wait for it to pass. Still in a state of shock, I shared my dream with her, and she said, "Well, it must have been because you saw the boys playing with pea shooters yesterday."

I thought about it for a minute, then said, "No, it wasn't." I remembered walking by the boys, but like most days at the time I was caught up in my grief over the breakup and not paying attention to them. Besides, even if I had seen the pea shooters it never would have occurred to me that the boys were putting straight pins in them! Thankfully, Shane was okay, but it left me with many questions about that dream and its significance. Little did I know I would have many other opportunities to explore the answers.

CHAPTER FOUR

DREAMS

Back when I first started having my strange dreams, there were no spiritual communities like we have now; there was no such thing as googling and no social media to connect with others who had experienced what I had. So, aside from telling Debbie the dream about her son, I kept them to myself. I also leaned once again on my astrological sign as an explanation. I needed an answer, and it was the only one that made any sense.

I eventually moved out of Debbie's apartment to a darling one-bedroom across the street and about a block away. The unit overlooked the pool and had leaded glass French doors leading to a beautiful balcony. I couldn't wait to plant flowers there. I even had a maple tree in a pot for privacy from the unit next door. I created my own little oasis where I could surround myself with the outside environment.

However, once I moved there, the dreams started up again and were soon coming nightly. I didn't understand why this was happening, but I realized I could no longer chalk it up to my astrological sign, as I knew other Pisces and they didn't have such experiences.

It started with a dream of me breaking a tooth on a popcorn kernel. The following day I remembered the dream but dismissed it as odd. As I was watching television that evening, I decided to make some popcorn, the dream from the night before gone from my thoughts. As I was munching down on the popcorn, I felt something happen inside my mouth. Oh my God, I thought. I broke a tooth! Still, I brushed it off as a coincidence. I mean, anyone could break a tooth, right?

When the movie was over I climbed into bed and fell fast asleep. In my dream, I saw the thumbnail on my right hand fly off! I had worn artificial fingernails for years but had never dreamt about them. It was very strange, and looking back now I wonder if someone on the other side was playing practical jokes on me. Of course, that thought didn't cross my mind at the time. The following day the sun was out, a rarity in the Seattle area, so I decided to go outside on the balcony and enjoy it. As I opened the door with my right hand, I saw the thumbnail fly right off my finger! I was in such shock that I couldn't even move; all I could do was stare at it. I had always done my manicures. The glue I used was new. Why was this happening?

Completely freaked out and, finally, realizing I had to talk to someone, I called my mom and shared the two stories with her, as well as the dream I'd had about Shane. Mom and I have always been very close and she's a great listener, but my stories disturbed her as well. How could I dream something, she asked, and then it happens the very next day? Was there a pattern to these dreams? I thought about it. Shane had swallowed the straight pin in the late morning; I broke my tooth in the evening; and I lost a fingernail in the early morning. There was no rhyme or reason to it. "If you have a dream about me," Mom said, "I don't want to know about it," and although she laughed I knew it made her slightly uncomfortable.

Great. Another dead-end. I decided it was no big deal, especially since aside from Shane swallowing the straight pin, the dreams had been about pretty minor things. I continued telling myself that until my nightmare the following evening.

Cheryl and I worked together at the Seattle Times newspaper. We had become quite close and even worked out at the gym together when we got off work. At the time Cheryl was training for the Miss Washington bodybuilding competition so when it was her turn we would add more weight onto the barbells. Her boyfriend was a sweetheart, but then Cheryl only dated great guys! He was a running back for the NFL team the Seattle Seahawks.

That evening was like any other. I hopped into bed at the usual time and fell into a deep sleep. Suddenly, I was watching Cheryl's boyfriend driving across the Evergreen Point Floating Bridge – also known as the "520-Bridge" – on his way from Seattle to his home in Bellevue. The bridge had grates in its mid-section, which would open and close to allow boats to pass through to the other side of Lake Washington.

In my dream, it was a rainy night, which is typical for Seattle, and as Cheryl's boyfriend reached the bridge's midpoint, he and the driver of another car started to lose control. Just as they were about to collide head-on, I shot up out of bed, trembling. This dream wasn't just about popcorn kernels and fingernails, and it shook me to my core. I knew I had to warn him.

The following day I called him as soon as I opened my eyes. He groggily answered the phone and told me he had been up late and was sleeping. I apologized for waking him and asked him to please contact me as soon as he woke up and to *not* leave the house. He said he would, so I waited for his call. There were no cell phones then, and it was important we talked. I didn't want anything to happen to him!

When I still hadn't heard from him by one p.m., I started getting antsy and decided to call again. I was so relieved when he answered! Now that I had his attention, how to begin? He didn't know about my dreams, so I just had to trust that he knew me well enough to realize that I wasn't a lunatic, or worse, engaged in some satanic behavior, and had his best interests at heart.

"I need to share something with you," I began slowly, "And I am not saying this to scare you or make you uncomfortable, but I want to tell you about a dream I had last night that involved you. In my dream, I saw you coming home from Seattle on the 520-Bridge, and as you hit the middle of the bridge where the grates are, I noticed that you and another car started to lose control and -"

He immediately cut me off, screaming, "That happened! That happened! It happened last night! Please don't tell Cheryl. I don't want her to worry, but it happened!"

Once again, I was horrified! Just when I thought I could stop something terrible from happening, my dream had occurred in real-time! What could possibly be the point of that?

After that, I became terrified to go to sleep for fear of what I might dream. I also remember begging God to please make the dreams go away.

"Please let me have a peaceful and restful night's sleep. Please, no dreams." That became my mantra for several nights and, thankfully, the dreams never returned.

CHAPTER FIVE

A DIFFERENT
KIND OF THERAPIST

By the mid-1980s, my biological clock was really starting to tick, and I was still having trouble in relationships. I was in counseling and had learned a lot, but my growth seemed to have plateaued. If someone had told me in 1969 that my week at the Christian camp in Canada would shape my future path, I would have thought they were crazy.

There is nothing more important than divine timing. All we have to do is recognize it and act. One day when I came into work I found a flyer on my desk, placed there by my friend Carol. The flyer read, "Trouble in relationships? Challenged with finances? I can help." The woman, Joy Tunell from Lynnwood, Washington, was an ordained minister, and since Carol, who I trusted implicitly, had already been to her I called and made an appointment for later that week. I needed answers, and I was praying Joy would be the one to unlock the door.

On the day of my appointment I drove to the address on the flyer and was surprised to find it was Joy's home. I was used to seeing my therapist in an office building, but again, I trusted Carol and figured that at this point I had nothing to lose.

Joy was a lovely lady, warm, inviting and I intuitively felt safe with her. She led me down a long hallway and into a very peaceful room. In the corner was a big Papasan-type chair, and she motioned for me to take a seat and relax. As I sunk back in the chair, she instructed me to get comfortable, close my eyes, and take several long deep breaths in through my nose and slowly out through my mouth.

"Have you been hypnotized before?" she asked.

"Yes. When I was in high school." I replied. I also warned her that I go deep and that she may have to "order" me to come out of it. During my senior year my psychology teacher had hypnotized me and I distinctly remembered feeling strange as I left his room and walked through the hallways to my next class. The walls were coming in on me, and the floor was moving in a wave-like pattern. I returned to his classroom, interrupted his class, and he took me into another room, counted down, and then back up, commanding me to return. It was definitely a little scary, certainly not something a public school teacher would even think of doing now. My concern was that if Joy hypnotized me I might still be "under" as I attempted to drive home.

Joy assured me that wouldn't happen; then while I relaxed in this big comfy chair, she explained that she would be counting backward, and I would descend deeper and deeper with each number. As she counted, she told me to imagine myself on a magic carpet. Sure enough, by the time she reached the count of three, I had attained a deep level of consciousness, yet I could still hear Joy say she was going to take me to a different land and another time. Even in my state, I thought, *What? Is she crazy? I do not understand what she means by this.* Then she had me step off the magic carpet and look down at my feet. My eyes were still closed, I wondered, so how did she expect me to see my feet?

"What do you see?" she asked.

"I don't see anything," I replied.

"Look again."

I hadn't taken my mental gaze off the ground where my feet were supposed to be, yet I saw nothing.

"Tell me what you see," she asked again.

"Nothing."

"Make it up."

I laughed to myself when she said that one. *Oh boy, What have I gotten myself into? This woman is a fake.*

"What do you see?" she asked again.

Rather than going around in circles, I did what she said. I made it up.

"Black shoes, the toes are rounded and . . ." Wow! I could not believe what was happening! I started to see them! ". . . there is a strap across the top of my foot and buckles."

"Good," she said, "Now, tell me what else you can see. Look up your body."

In complete and total disbelief, I continued to describe my feet, legs and the dress I was wearing. How could I be seeing these things?

"Good," Joy encouraged, "Now, I want you to look out and tell me what you see."

That's when I noticed a red brick building with stairs in front of me. The building was old. When I crossed the street to walk up the stairs, I felt like I was in Europe, though, I had never been there. I just had this inner knowing that I was no longer in the United States. When I went inside, I saw a dance studio. A man I knew to be my husband was to the left, and I remember him smiling. Our daughter Jennifer, who we called Jenny, was happily skipping around the room.

"Okay," Joy said. "I want you to fast forward to later in that lifetime."

I started crying and screamed, "My husband died! He died in an accident!" I don't know how, but he died, he was gone, and Jenny and I were alone. I told her, "This is not good."

"Okay, I am going to put you on the magic carpet and take you to a different land and a different time."

Oh, thank God, I thought. I was at a loss for words. I had come to Joy for help, and instead I was more heartbroken than ever. *Deb, focus. Just focus and trust,* I said to myself.

I had several other experiences with Joy that day, and they too were extremely upsetting.

"I want you to be with this for one week, then come back and I will show you happy lifetimes," she assured me.

What? Is she kidding me? But what else was I to do? I had no other choice but to trust her. Thankfully, she was right.

Whether you believe in reincarnation or not is entirely up to you, just like my experiences with Jesus. It is my truth. It's my story. I know there will be backlash, against me and possibly my family as well, from others who feel this is blasphemy, and for that I am truly sorry. Yet I cannot ignore what He tells me, and that is to share this. If I don't, how will I answer God when it's my time to cross the veil? I cannot explain these things, I can only tell you about my experiences and assure you that I am not making them up.

Indeed, if Joy had told me before my first session that she was going to regress me, I would never have agreed to it out of fear. Boy, am I glad she didn't! My time with her was not only eye-opening, it laid out a new path before me. She started teaching classes, and I was eager to sign up and soak in her knowledge, hoping to find answers about myself and the experiences I'd had when I was younger. However, I was still reluctant to share my time with Jesus, which is strange, considering I shared just about everything with people, including stories about all the men I dated. The ladies at the newspaper loved hearing about my weekend escapades, but surely they would have been surprised to learn about this part of my life, just as one of my spiritual teachers was shocked when I told him I was a union organizer.

"What?" he'd said, looking at me in amazement.

"I know, I know," I replied. "There are two sides to me, and after all, that is about being of service, too."

When Joy told me that she was having a one-day channeling workshop, I was intrigued but cautious. This was at a time when American spiritual teacher J.Z. Knight, who lived in Tacoma, Washington became known for channeling a spiritual entity named Ramtha. Initially, I thought the woman must be crazy, because how can that happen? My curiosity was piqued when Linda Evans, one of the stars of the TV show Dynasty, became her friend and Shirley MacLaine came out as a new-ager, but channeling an entity of unknown origin still didn't seem conceivable. I would eventually realize that, like reincarnation, it only seems that way until you meet someone you trust who can speak from personal experience. However, at the time I had no knowledge of this phenomenon and told Joy I didn't want any part of it.

Joy smiled. "Trust me. That will not happen. That isn't what I teach."

I did trust her, so I signed up for the class and ended up learning about another gift I didn't realize I had. Joy explained that since I could see my own past lives during regression I could see others' previous incarnations as well. She was simply helping to awaken me and my classmates to the ability.

What? Really? But how? I couldn't fathom this being possible.

I still didn't know how it worked, but I learned that Joy was right. We all sat in a circle on the floor in her living room. There was a smaller circle inside ours with friends who volunteered so we could practice. I didn't think about it at the time, because I was just learning and focused on what I had to do, but as I gained wisdom I often wondered what those volunteers experienced that day.

I remember going into meditation, placing my hands on this one young lady, and being completely amazed at what I was able to see. It was as if I had flipped on the television and the screen was right before me, but my eyes were closed! I started seeing pictures of a field covered in daisies. All I saw were these beautiful yellow daisies. I continued to describe it to her in every minute detail while waiting for the next slide or picture to appear; however, it was as if the vision was stuck on the pause button. All I kept seeing were daisies, so I continued describing them, down to every last petal.

"Okay, sixty more seconds. Time to wrap it up," Joy said.

I remember shaking my head from side to side. All I could tell her was this glorious field of daisies; the sun was shining, and I could see the sky. It was nothing but daisies.

"Okay. Time is up!"

I opened my eyes to see this young lady crying. Tears were streaming down her cheeks.

"Did that mean anything to you?" I asked.

"Yes," she said, smiling.

"Okay, time to move on to the next person," Joy said as we continued around the room.

Later, I realized that what I was seeing were their past lives. I was amazed by this experience, and each person I practiced with validated the process. Yet it was the young boy fishing that I would continue to wonder about for years.

I remember sitting across from this man, holding his hands, and telling him about the vision before me. There was a young boy walking down a rutted dirt road with grass growing in the middle. He carried a fishing pole, and he was happy. His hair was brown, straight, with a "Dennis the Menace" cowlick bobbing with each step. The sun was shining brightly, and I could hear birds singing. Tall, wheat-colored grass surrounded him on each side of the road.

"There has got to be a lake, a river, or a stream, but I've yet to see it," I said.

I told the man everything I was seeing, Then, as I mentioned that he also carried a fishing basket with a strap over his shoulder, I heard, *Tell him he's got eggs in his basket.*

What? I thought. *That has nothing to do with this story.* But as I continued telling him what I was seeing, the voice came in louder: *Tell him he has eggs in his basket!*

No! I internally argued back, *That has nothing to do with the story!*

At that moment, Joy interrupted. "Okay, sixty more seconds. Time to wrap it up."

Several decibels louder, the voice shouted, *TELL HIM HE HAS EGGS IN THE BASKET!*

I remember picking up the man's hands in frustration, then gently putting them down on his knees.

"I am supposed to tell you that you have eggs in your basket."

At that very moment, the screen in my head went blank, and the image disappeared!

"Did that mean anything to you?" I asked the man.

"Not until you told me I had eggs in my basket."

Unfortunately, I never got the opportunity to ask him what the eggs were about. It is a regret I have to this day.

Those sessions and classes with Joy gave me the foundation for creating a better life. When you see where you have come from, it is easier to know where you are going. That is why it was vital to learn hypnosis and how to facilitate past life regressions. It was the final ticket I needed to leave the insecurities of Debbie behind and become the Debra I was meant to be.

CHAPTER SIX

MEETING MY PRINCE

By the summer of 1987, I was thirty-three and feeling as if life was passing me by. My mom told me I had to get out more. "He's not going to come knocking on your door," she would say. However, I knew having a man in my life wasn't the answer. I believed at the time that if I surrounded myself with things like jewelry and clothing, I would be satisfied. I even had a '79 Arctic White Mercedes 450SL convertible with red leather interior and chrome wire wheels. It was my dream car. However, after only owning it one year, the "high" wore off. I had everything I wanted but these things didn't make me happy or feel complete. Something was *missing*. I knew I needed to pay attention to the training from Joy, quiet my mind, and *listen*.

At the time, there was all this chatter about something called the Harmonic Convergence. This significant shift in consciousness was supposed to be on August 16, and was closely aligned with the planets in the solar system. A global peace meditation was to be held at several places around the world. The more I *listened*, the more I intuitively knew I needed to take a solo trip to Cannon Beach on the Oregon Coast. My dear friend and mentor Kate Wright had told me numerous times how lovely and quaint the town was, but I had never been. Now, given everything she had taught me and the fact I felt best by water, I *sensed a need* to go and experience it for myself.

Still, I was reluctant as I packed my car that weekend, as I had never been on vacation alone before. Any trepidation I felt immediately disappeared the moment I arrived in Cannon Beach; in fact, as I drove into town, I was surprised that tears started streaming down my cheeks. I had never experienced a feeling of belonging like that in my life, and though I couldn't explain it, it was as if I had been there before.

Not yet ready to commit to a move, I started visiting Cannon Beach every weekend. I remember one day crying in the shower because I couldn't go that Saturday due to commitments. I felt stuck. I knew Cannon Beach was home. It was as if someone had screwed a large bolt into my chest. There was a circle sticking out with a rope through the ring, and it was tugging at me; the rope was pulling me to go to the place I knew was home.

Trusting my intuition, I finally decided to take a sabbatical from my job at the newspaper and move to the Oregon Coast to be *one with the ocean*.

You can only imagine what my family thought. I felt terrible for my parents. They had been through enough with me already, now here I was again, going off on another tangent. "Why on earth," my mother said, "would you sell the car you've always dreamed of having and leave your job?" I didn't have an answer, at least not one I could articulate. It's not always easy to explain that yes, though you may have a terrific job and a great car, you aren't satisfied and know something is missing. I certainly couldn't tell them I'd *heard* that I was supposed to go.

I put an ad in the newspaper to sell my beloved Mercedes convertible, telling the people who inquired that I wouldn't just sell it to anybody. Looking back, I have to laugh. Who says that? But the car had been my dream, and I wanted to make sure that it went to someone who would love and appreciate it as much as I did.

I remember this one stunning older woman who came for a test drive. When she slid into the driver's seat, her perfectly styled white hair stood out, and I just knew she would be the one to buy the car. Sure enough, she put five hundred dollars down and said she would have her mechanic look at it that Friday. It didn't give me much time as I was moving the following Monday, but I knew the car would be hers. In fact, because of that, I never responded to the messages other potential buyers left on my answering machine.

One day I answered my phone and heard a man shout, "Why haven't you returned my calls?"

"Excuse me? Who is this?"

"It's Bill Ewing. I have been leaving you messages that I wanted to see your car, but you never called me back!"

"Oh! I'm sorry. I have been busy packing to move," I replied, "Besides, the car is sold."

"What!? It's *sold*?"

"Well, not exactly. The woman purchasing the vehicle is having her mechanic look at it on Friday, but I know everything will be fine."

"Well, the deal could fall through, you know," Bill said.

What? I knew everything was in alignment with my path. Why did he have to put doubt in my mind? Though I was slightly annoyed, I agreed to show him the car, just in case.

Oddly enough, Bill and I had an interesting conversation. After we hung up, I thought of something else to tell him and called back, but the phone went to voice mail. I left a message, and when Bill returned my call he apologized and said he had been in his hot tub.

Hmmm, that's interesting. My thoughts continued to drift as we talked a bit more about the car. There was something about him that intrigued me, but I forced myself to return to reality. *Deb, you're off to be one with the ocean. You don't want a relationship right now,* I told myself.

The next evening, he came to test drive the car. He seemed nice enough, but not what I had envisioned in my mind. It's not that he wasn't attractive, he just didn't fit my type. I often dated men who looked as if they'd walked off a romance novel or a magazine cover. In fact, a couple of them had. But again, there was just something about him, and I had to remind myself, *He's here to look at the car!*

We went for a test drive that turned out to be a little longer than I thought, but I enjoyed Bill's company. Finally, we returned to my apartment, and he said he would call Friday night to see if the other interested party had decided to purchase it.

Friday came, and the lady bought the car. I had tears as I saw it leave the driveway one last time. Selling my dream car to take off to Cannon Beach and be "one with the ocean" – what was I thinking? Just when I started to think I was going crazy, I felt that old pull in the center of my chest again, and I knew the doubt would pass. I could always return to Washington and my job, get another apartment, and buy another car!

I waited, but that night I didn't hear from Bill Ewing.

When Saturday came and went and he still hadn't called, I just chalked it up to "men" and thought it was a good thing I was leaving. My *picker* was still off, and I wasn't a good judge of character. C'est la vie!

On Sunday I finished packing as I had to work on Monday and be out of my apartment by Tuesday. I was busy trying to wrap things up for my leave at work, and the phone was ringing off the hook. Another call came in, and I answered, "Advertising, this is Debra, can you hold please?" Not waiting for a response, I put the caller on hold.

After about two minutes, I picked up the phone, "Thank you for waiting. This is Debra. Can I help you?"

"Where are you!" a man said with frustration in his voice.

"Excuse me? Advertising, this is Debra. How can I help you?"

"Wait! Do you mean to tell me I have been calling this phone number since Friday night?"

"Excuse me?"

"This is Bill Ewing. I thought you had already left town because this was the number I have been calling since Friday night."

I laughed and said, "No, this is my work number," but inside I was sighing with relief. Okay, maybe my *picker* isn't entirely off.

"Did you sell the car?" he asked.

"Yes, I did."

"Well, it was a beauty. Congratulations. You know, I enjoyed meeting you and wanted to take you out for dinner, but I guess that won't happen now."

"No, I leave tomorrow," I told him.

"Well, do you have a phone number in Cannon Beach where I can reach you?"

"I have a post office box," I said, "and I can call you once I get a telephone."

"Great," he said. "I would appreciate that."

And that, dear readers, is the story of how I met my prince! Sorry, Mom, this time you were wrong. He *did* come knocking on my door!

The significance of all this wasn't lost on me. If I hadn't *listened* to my intuition, I wouldn't have sold my car, and I would never have met Bill. There truly is a reason for everything. I find myself laughing as I write this, because Jesus is talking to me again, *saying, "Trust the process."*

This brings to mind the concept of ego. I never thought of myself as an egotistical person, I just liked nice things. Who doesn't? But over the years ego has come to mean something very different, and the best way I can explain it is with the acronym Edging God Out. When we get caught up in those *things* that we think are making us happy, we have to work harder to pay for them, and then we get bored with those items and want something more significant, newer, brighter, and shinier. It's a vicious cycle, and I wasted so much time and money on *things*. In hindsight, I wish I had approached life differently, but they were all lessons to get me to where I am now. I believe the pain and anguish I went through is worth something; it's worth sharing so women can stop replaying the broken record, feel empowered and start living their best life! That is the book I thought I was writing, that is, until Jesus began popping into my head!

Bill came to Cannon Beach for our first date, and I found myself sharing my spiritual experiences with him. I felt it was important to explain so he could fully understand why I'd thrown caution to the wind, left my job, and moved to Cannon Beach. I know it didn't appear like a rational thing to do!

"I am searching… " I began, "I have had these experiences that I can't explain…" I then proceeded to tell him about my visitations, including the one with my grandfather on the other side.

At the time Bill didn't seem to understand and, in retrospect, he probably thought I was a little crazy, yet six weeks after our first date we had fallen in love, so he asked me to come back to Seattle and move in with him. I had been searching. Cannon Beach served its purpose.

"Don't tell anybody that you talk to dead people," he cautioned.

I laughed and said, "Okay," And though I didn't really view it as talking to dead people, I kept my abilities hidden, until now.

CHAPTER SEVEN

MY DAD'S PASSING & VISIT

When I was a young adult, and certainly when I was growing up, psychics were frowned upon. I remember hearing people say it was the work of the devil and something you don't mess with. It's "voodoo." Of course, since then I have realized that psychic abilities are *gifts,* which allowed me, after decades of secrecy, to share mine so that I can bring some measure of peace and comfort to those who are grieving or are waiting to cross over. I have seen the other side, and it is so magical and incredible it's hard to put into words. I have also been studying the afterlife for the past six years so I have additional knowledge I can share with others and hopefully eliminate fear. That is my soul's purpose.

Bill and I got married in 1989. I was thirty-five, much older than I had anticipated, but I was glad I had waited until I knew it was right. Divorce was not an option for me, and intuitively I always knew I would only walk down the aisle one time. I also had great role models in my parents, who had enjoyed forty-eight years of wedded bliss. Most importantly, I was coming from a place of contentment and self-love, and had found a man who was as well.

35

In December of 1991 our daughter Erica was born, and it was the most awe-inspiring time of our lives. Creating a human together is such a humbling and miraculous experience. Our world revolved around her. Nothing mattered except being as good a mother as possible. I took parenting classes and read books on how to best support and empower her. I wanted Erica raised with confidence. If you think about it, babies come into the world as perfect humans; it's through their parents or other outside influences that insecurities and self-doubt enter. Wouldn't it be a beautiful world if we never had to deal with any of that? I didn't even think about my spirituality then. Being a mom was something I always wanted, so she was my entire focus. Who knew I could have both?

As Erica grew up, I found it interesting that out of all her books she loved her children's bible most of all. I would read it to her every night before she fell asleep, and when I finished she'd tell me to start over from the beginning. I didn't think anything of it; I figured she just liked the stories.

Erica was a very bright child, and people often thought she was older than her age because she articulated her words so well. One day when she was about two years old, Bill was driving through downtown Seattle. She was in her car seat in the back, sucking on her binky. As we passed the Seattle Center, she noticed a skate park, removed the binky and made a comment. I wish I could remember what she said, but it was so profound and caught me so off guard that I turned around in the passenger seat and asked, "Erica, how do you know that?"

She replied, "Because from when I was up in heaven before I was born."

I was stunned, and Bill yelled at me, "What are you teaching her?"

I looked at him and laughed. "You think I am teaching a two-year-old about reincarnation? Are you kidding me!"

To this day, I regret not asking her questions, even if to just say, "Tell me more." At the time, it simply didn't occur to me.

Erica was four years old when my father got sick. They were very close, and Erica would crawl up onto the hospital bed hospice had placed in my parents' home and snuggle with him. She even helped feed him. Though we all thought it was cute and endearing, we were unaware of the special bond they were creating.

It was Christmas Eve, 1995. Bill and I decided to spend the night at my parents' house – we even made a point of letting Santa know where we would be. My dad was in a coma-like state on Christmas Day. We would go in and speak to him, but he didn't respond. We knew the time was near. We were fortunate enough to have a lovely hospice nurse stay with us. I knew God sent her because she had the same last name as my parents.

My husband and my father also shared an incredible bond. Bill had lost his father when he was in his early twenties, so he never experienced a relationship with him as an adult. However, he did have a lot of great times with my dad, talking about sports, playing cribbage, and discussing building and remodeling plans. But I'll never forget what Bill told my father that day.

"I will be there, Jim. I will look after Maxine. Don't worry," he said. I appreciated him saying that he would care for my mother, as well as me and Erica. He loved my father, too.

After our holiday get-together, everyone returned home, except for me. At four a.m. on December 26, the nurse woke my mother and me up, telling us it was time. Mom called my brother, and he immediately came over. We gathered around my father's bed, holding his hand, telling him how much we loved him. I remember my mother saying, "It's okay, Jim. It's okay to go." Thirty minutes later, he was gone.

Previously I had learned that my father chose to be cremated, and I was having a hard time with it. *What?* I thought. *He wants to be burned to a crisp?* My granddad and grandma were in a cemetery together, and I'd assumed my parents would do the same. I had a place to go and talk to them. I usually brought flowers, except for Christmas when I got a small living tree for their grave. Finally, I spoke with my minister at Unity Church, as well as my friend Kate, both of whom helped ease my fears. Kate told me it was my father's wish, and I had to come to terms with it as it would make passing easier for him. I wouldn't say I liked it, but I did tell him it was okay. The morning of his passing, I asked the funeral director to please save a lock of his hair for me, and he did. I was then able to let my daddy go.

Losing a parent is so difficult. It's as if a piece of you has left with them. I remember going outside as they escorted my father away. The morning was still pitch black except for one bright star. I stared at it for the longest time while I mentally spoke to my daddy. "Remember what I said, Dad, go to the white light. Don't be afraid. Mom and Pop will be there. Go to the light, Dad. We will all be together again someday. I love you. Always remember how much I love you. Thank you for everything you did for me; thank you for everything you gave me. We had such a great life. I love you, Dad."

I spent that night with Mom. I didn't want her to be alone; besides, we were both grieving and wondering what our new normal would look like. In the morning she told me she had heard my dad call out her name in the middle of the night. She'd replied, "What, Jim?" but that was all she remembered.

After my father's passing, our lives completely changed. There was a big hole in our world with no way to fill it. Mom spent time with friends; she would go shopping and, eventually, she decided to do some volunteer work. She also joined a grief support group to meet others who were going through the same experience. That support group was her lifeline. Until someone walks in your shoes, they can never fully understand what you are going through. Her married friends tried to be comforting by saying, "I know how you're feeling," but they didn't. They could only imagine what it must be like to lose your partner of forty-eight years.

After his passing, Erica continued to talk about her "Gran-Gran." She also spoke of dreams she had about him. Given my own experiences, I believe they were not just dreams, but *visits* so he could check on her, letting her know that he wasn't gone, just as Jesus visited me as a teen. That special bond between Erica and my father is still there to this day. It is evident in her computer passwords, on her wedding day, and items of his that she holds close to her heart. Truly, we don't ever die; we merely change form as we move to the other side while living in the hearts of those we leave behind.

As the months passed, I continued speaking to my dad, asking him to visit me. The comment of a well-meaning coworker – "If your father doesn't accept Jesus Christ as his Lord and Savior he won't be allowed into heaven" – was haunting me, and I had to know that he was okay.

My Dad was a good man. He was kind, loving, funny, and volunteered his time to be of service to others in our community; yet, without proof it was hard for him to believe. The Jesus I knew wouldn't deny him entrance into heaven, yet I couldn't help but be scared. This coworker read from the bible, so what if they knew something I didn't? I just needed my doubts to be put to rest.

In October 1996, ten months after he left the earth, Dad came to me in a dream, and it had the same vividness as the other visitations I had experienced. I saw myself walking with this young man. From my peripheral vision, I could see his legs in stride with mine, and though I never looked at his face I trusted him and felt comfortable. We were in a park so lovely there are no words in the English dictionary that do it justice. The flowers were so vibrant, they were glistening, kind of like those GIFs you click on and they start sparkling. The hues of purple were indescribable. The grass was thick and the most vivid green. The trees were big and strong. I could hear birds singing, but I didn't see them. Instead, I was soaking in the vibrance of the setting.

I continued walking along a path with this young man. I had no fear, yet I didn't know where or why I was dreaming this. Finally, he turned to the left, and off in the distance on a grassy knoll underneath a weeping willow tree was my brother Jim, my dad, and my mother lying on their backs, napping. The young man walked me over to them, and as I approached I saw my father's eyes *pop open*! Startled, I quickly took a step back, but Dad smiled at me and said, "Do you remember that talk you had with me about Heaven?"

I nodded my head and said, "Yes."

"You were exactly right. You'll see." Then he closed his eyes, and I woke up hysterical.

I had asked, and my dad found a way to come. He was about ten years younger than when he passed, and healthy. My mother and Jim never opened their eyes, but I remember thinking, "Does that mean they will pass before me?" That notion bothered me. I am older than my brother, and I just naturally assumed he would outlive me. Then I read about visits, and how those across the veil create an environment where you feel comfortable. It all made sense. I only wish I had looked at the young man who was guiding me. I am confident he was my brother Steven, who passed as an infant.

A year later, in the fall of 1997, something entirely unexpected happened. My mother met a widower in the grief support group she attended and there was instant chemistry. Mom acted like a schoolgirl, and though they were perfect for each other I had some things to work through. No one could ever replace my dad, and Dick, Mom's new boyfriend, assured me that was not his intention.

After we got to know Dick, we started to embrace him. He was kind, gentle, loving, and he adored my mother. We felt very fortunate that he came into our lives. Finally, Mom had a reason to smile again, and love and joy filled her heart. It was a different kind of love, but it was profound. I even remember being a little bit envious, as her life was now more exciting than mine! It reminded me you have to continually work on your relationship. You need to communicate, take nothing for granted, schedule date nights, and remember why you fell in love to help get you through the rough times.

CHAPTER EIGHT

MESSAGES

One morning on my way to work, I kept getting these *messages* or *downloads.* They started as I pulled up to the street light just before getting onto the freeway. We lived on Lake Burien, so it was easier to take the Viaduct into town instead of driving down Interstate-5. It was one way I could avoid the traffic and be on time for work.

As I was waiting for the light to turn green, I heard, *Go straight.*

What? No! I'm taking the Viaduct, I argued silently.

As the light turned green, I heard it again – "GO STRAIGHT!" – only this time the voice was shouting.

I remember letting out a deep sigh and shouting back, "OKAY! I'll go straight!" Maybe, I thought, there was a backup or an accident on the Viaduct and by going straight and taking Interstate-5 I could avoid it.

As I continued driving, my radar was up. I never took this route to work, and I was still wondering why the voice had been so insistent about it.

I quickly merged onto the interstate and settled in the far-left lane as I now needed a few extra minutes to arrive at work on time. There was an old pickup truck in front of me, and for some reason it felt better to keep a good car length between us. Keeping to the posted speed limit of sixty miles an hour, I turned on some music, relaxed and got into the flow of traffic.

Suddenly, the pickup truck swerved sharply to the left, hitting the cement guard rail and flipping over in front of me! The vehicle ended up horizontal in the lane with the driver hanging by his seatbelt upside down, looking out the driver's window at my car headed straight for him!

I immediately downshifted and slammed on my brakes, coming to a stop within ten feet of the driver's side window. I then jumped out of the car to check on the two men in the pickup cab, only to find them laughing hysterically! Me? I was trembling and shaking and trying to catch my breath. I could not believe what had just happened! That's when the driver told me the car in front of him slammed on their brakes, and as he tried to stop, he hit the guard rail and flipped. Debris cluttered the road from the bed of the pickup, including quite a few empty beer cans. No, I don't think they were drinking at seven a.m. – the cans were probably from some other time – but I helped them pick everything up just before the police arrived. I gave the officer my name and number and said I had to get to work, then I was off.

When I arrived at work, I had time to breathe and reflect on my commute. Beyond a shadow of a doubt, I knew that I was supposed to drive to work that day on I-5 to keep those men safe. Everyone else on the commute was in their own little world, drinking their coffee or eating breakfast in their car, as so many of us typically are on a drive we take so often we could do it with our eyes closed. I now know why the voice screamed, "GO STRAIGHT!" If I hadn't listened to that little voice, the men probably would have died that morning, or at least the driver. No one would have been laughing then!

Intuition is funny. We all have it; we just need to learn to tune into it. But where does it come from? Are they messages from our guardian angels, God, our loved ones across the veil, or all of the above? I can tell you one thing: ninety-seven percent of the time, I listen to it. Whenever I don't listen, I wind up wishing I had!

One morning in 1998, Bill rolled over in bed and said, "What do you think about moving to Arizona?' I was shocked to hear him ask this. I loved living on Lake Burien. I especially enjoyed the mornings when I could hear the ducks on the lake if the dog next door wasn't barking at them, causing a nuisance. On the other hand, I was sick of the Seattle rain, and we had a condominium in Old Town Scottsdale that I hated leaving every time we had to return home for work. I remember the countless times we had landed at Sea-Tac to rain sleeting against the windows of the plane and the tears streaming down my cheeks. This was not quality of life to me.

It was Bill's turn to be shocked when I quickly said, "Okay!" He had assumed that after spending my entire life in the Northwest I would at least have to give it some thought. I didn't. We lived on a lake but I looked at it more than I was in it; I drove a convertible but I could count the number of times the top had been down. I was so over the rain, umbrellas, raincoats, wet shoes that tracked pine needles in the house, and damp hair – ugh. Mom was with Dick, so she was okay, and my husband had fulfilled his vow to my father. Erica would be starting the first grade, so a move would arguably be less traumatizing than if she were older, and I had twenty-six years in at the newspaper, so why not! The decision was so easy, in part, because of my dad's passing. It had shown me how short life truly is, and how essential it is to *live* and be *happy*. I was tired of being miserable.

We sold our home within the first week, and by May 1998 we were packed and headed to the Valley of the Sun. It was sad to leave the lake and the West Coast, and I wouldn't get to visit Cannon Beach as often, but I viewed it as a new adventure. I also knew Sedona was only ninety minutes away. While it's not the water or near a lake, it's a very spiritual place, with several vortexes, breathtaking red rock buttes, and other new things for me to explore.

— CHAPTER NINE —

THE SUNNY SOUTH IS CALLING!

Living in the two-bedroom condo was not ideal, and fortunately, we found a house right away. When I reflect on that day, I remember feeling that my father guided me to this home. We had been driving through a neighborhood in the school district we chose for our daughter to attend. We drove up and down the streets and were getting ready to leave the subdivision when I intuitively told Bill to take a left.

"Let's go down this street one more time."

He did as I asked, and I casually glanced from side to side, checking out the houses. Then I looked straight ahead and saw a man, pounding a For Sale By Owner sign into the lawn!

"Stop!" I yelled, so Bill pulled over. We got out and spoke to the man in the yard.

"Go on in," he said, motioning to the front door as he left us and entered through the garage.

Upon entering, I just knew. I looked at Bill and said, "This is it!"

"What? We haven't even looked at the house! We're still in the entryway."

Though we had been together for years, Bill sometimes had to be reminded of my intuitive gifts.

"This is it!!" I repeated.

"Okay, but keep your mouth shut. You will ruin any bargaining power."

After that comment, I had to laugh. I already knew this was our home.

The owners were waiting in the family room for us. As I walked into the kitchen, I felt my father's presence. I looked out the window above the sink, and it was perfect. The backyard was all grass. This is ideal, I thought. I could design it exactly how I wanted! That's when I knew without a doubt that Dad guided us there.

Ever since I was a little girl, my dream was to have my daddy build a home for me. I used to go to the job sites with him and help out with sweeping and cleaning up. I remember one time I even helped him stain the windowsills. He told me he had to pay people nine dollars an hour to do that work, and I felt so good that I was saving him money. I had the gene. I knew how to use tools and build things. I was Jim Moore's daughter, and this was the house where he wanted me to live.

Bill and I walked down the hall to view the rest of the home. It was perfect – twenty-one hundred square feet with a good-sized living room, formal dining area, three bedrooms, two bathrooms, and even a den.

"I love it!" I exclaimed.

"Shhh…"

We walked back into the family room, and Bill asked the gentleman, "How much?"

"Two hundred and twenty thousand," he said.

I was shocked. We had just sold our place in Seattle for five hundred thousand! I couldn't believe we could get this newly remodeled home for less than half that.

Bill nodded his head without emotion. I looked at him and said, "Bill, where did you ever think we would find a home that I would be happy with for two-hundred thousand?" He looked at me, laughed, and said, "You're right." We talked about the home some more and offered two hundred and fifteen thousand cash, which the owners accepted. We also met their son and daughter-in-law, who lived across the street. They had an older daughter named Erika and another daughter who was Erica's age named Mandy. This was perfect! We had found our home! Thank you, Daddy!

At the time, Bill and I were both retired and living off our investments. We had tried our hand at day trading school, only to realize that we were more comfortable buying and holding stock. We had catastrophic health insurance for the time being, but we knew one of us had to get a real job with health benefits. My sister-in-law worked for America West, the hometown airline, so I thought, why not apply there? Fortunately, I got hired, and though the pay was deplorable the health insurance was fantastic!

We quickly settled into our new home, and several months later I started my training at America West. Sedona became my new go-to place, over the next five years I would take many trips there. I enjoyed taking out-of-town guests, but I especially liked driving up alone with the top down, hair blowing in the breeze while listening to my Robin Miller music. It was my escape where I could meditate, go within, and be one with the energy of the vortexes and God. I always hated leaving and dreamed of having a home or a spiritual retreat where guests could participate in classes and connect with others of like consciousness. In the meantime, I created an idyllic setting right in my backyard, just as I had envisioned when we first saw the house. I was happy.

One morning in 2003, I had just gotten out of the shower when I heard a *voice*.

"Stand in front of the mirror with your hands behind your head."

Yes, I thought that was odd, not the voice (I was used to that), but the message! I thought, smiling, *Who does that? Who stands in front of the mirror with their hands behind their head?*

So, I obeyed, looked in the mirror, clasped my hands together behind my head, and noticed a dimple under my right areola. I looked at it, felt it with my left hand, felt for a lump, had my husband look, and couldn't find anything, so we forgot about it. *Probably just cellulite,* I thought. I had turned forty-nine in March, so I was sure that was what it was. The old body was changing!

Two months later, in May, I had my annual checkup with my gynecologist. She examined me and said that everything looked great and she would schedule my yearly mammogram. She then asked, "Is there anything else you need to discuss?"

I said, "Yes. I want to show you something." I removed the gown and placed my right hand behind my head. "Look. There's a dimple. It is probably just cellulite because I'm almost fifty, but this is the only way you can see it, and I wanted to show it to you." Honestly, I wasn't concerned. My brother Jim has dimples in his cheeks, and it looked just like those.

She said, "Okay, let's schedule your mammogram. It's probably nothing but let's have a follow-up appointment afterward."

I admit I was a little nervous when I went for the mammogram; however, they have a breast clinic there, and I received the results right away. The nurse came out with the paperwork, handed it to me, and said, "Everything is normal. We will see you in one year."

Whew, as I breathed a sigh of relief. Thank you, God!

The following week I was back at the doctor with the report. She examined me again and said, "Debra, I want a breast surgeon to examine you."

Now I was pissed! "What! Why?"

"Because we need to know what is tugging at that skin,' she said.

"But my mammogram is negative!"

"I know and it is probably nothing," she said reassuringly, "but we need to be positive."

Well, you already know where this is going. Yep. I had breast cancer. How can that be? My mammogram was negative, the ultrasound they did was negative, but then came the MRI, and sure enough, the damn lump was hiding behind my areola. What the hell?? I was in total shock. My family was scared. I was scared. Cancer? But I am so healthy!

It is terrifying for any woman or man who has traveled this path. Fear starts to creep in. You start thinking of things left undone. Our daughter was only eleven! I wanted to live to see her graduate high school, get married and have children! No, this isn't happening to me!

Only it was.

I went through the barrage of appointments, surgery, and radiation for four weeks instead of five because I'd signed up for a clinical trial in which they used radiation internally before stitching me up. This made more sense – attack the area where you take the tumor from in hopes of killing any minuscule cells left behind, right? Then, unexpectedly came the chemotherapy conversation. I was furious about that. I didn't want to lose all my hair! I can laugh now as that sounds completely ridiculous, but it's where I was at the time.

Because I was having trouble emotionally with this, my doctor had me see an oncology therapist. He thought she might be able to help me. Initially, I was annoyed. She had long thick reddish, auburn hair almost down to her waist, and here I was afraid of being bald with stubble. I tried to get past it, but understandably I felt like I would lose my femininity. The doctor's mantra kept playing in my mind: *You are only forty-nine with an eleven-year-old at home.* That is all the doctor had to say for me to agree to chemotherapy; however, I was still afraid.

After our consult, Pauline told me that she wanted to use a different type of therapy on me.

"I don't do this with just anybody," she added.

"Well, I beat to a different drummer, so go for it!"

During these sessions, Pauline would sit behind me and place her hands on my shoulders before she started. Then, with soft music playing in the background, she would take me on a guided meditation, all the while keeping her hands on my shoulders. She was right. This therapy was different and unexpected. Sometimes I would go to Cannon Beach, and other times I would go to Sedona. I found these sessions with her highly relaxing, and I looked forward to them.

On one of my visits, I had the most profound thing happen. I had not experienced this since I was a teenager. My eyes were closed, my head bowed, and off to my right was Jesus! I was in complete shock! Oh my God! I had not seen Him since high school, thirty-three years earlier! I sat there in awe, staring at Him as tears started to stream down my cheeks, when all of a sudden, Pauline asked, "Who is that man standing off to your right with the long brown hair?"

At that moment, I started sobbing uncontrollably. "You see Him, too?" I exclaimed, shocked. This was unbelievable! How could I have forgotten? He has always been with me!

And that was the beginning of my reconnection with my friend. If Pauline, a highly respected oncology therapist at a prominent hospital, could see Him, then I knew I wasn't making it up. I mean, I knew I wasn't, but after all these years without visits, you start to wonder. Thank you, God! At that very moment, all fear was gone, never to return. I knew I would survive.

My father also appeared during one of the meditations. I had been feeling the effects of the chemo, and he motioned me over where he had a lovely comfortable cot for me to relax on. It had a thin mattress, and he covered me with a light blanket. I found it interesting that he would show up in meditation; then again, Jesus had, so why couldn't my dad? It brought me comfort just knowing he was there.

Now that my mind was at peace, I decided to attend church the following Sunday. I found a Unity Church in Phoenix because I used to go to one not far from my home in Washington. During the meditation, I had a conversation with God, "Okay, so I have breast cancer. What do you want me to do with it?"

His message came through loud and clear: "Educate other women." Then, right on the heels of that, He added, "There are things more important than money."

Now that was interesting, I thought, as Bill and I had been day trading and were on margin when the market crashed overnight. We had lost just about everything.

After receiving that message, I started speaking out on breast cancer. I told women the keyword is *change*, not a *lump*. I had found this dimple in March but waited until my annual exam in May to go because it wasn't a lump, and I had breast cancer! I made it my mission to openly discuss it, let women see the surgery, touch the radiated skin, and ask questions. Knowledge is power, and I knew this is what God wanted me to do.

I also started volunteering with a program sponsored by the American Cancer Society called Look Good, Feel Better. It's a terrific program where numerous cosmetic companies donate their products so women can feel more beautiful while going through chemotherapy. I had enjoyed the class as a participant, so I thought I would volunteer as a survivor to bring hope to those struggling so they would see that they can survive too. We watched a video about hair coverings and wigs that was very helpful, not to mention the makeup kit that was fun to play with. Chemo also makes you lose your eyebrows and lashes and this class taught them valuable tricks to compensate and make them feel better about their appearance.

I remember one evening, there was a lady who was in the middle of chemotherapy. She had a port, which is something thankfully I wasn't required to have, and I noticed it just didn't look right. Now, I am not a doctor, and I have no medical background, but my intuition said something was wrong. "Has it always been red like that?" I asked her.

"No," she replied, "It happened today after my treatment. We live an hour from here, so we went out for a late lunch and had been waiting for this class tonight before going home. My husband is sitting over there," she added as she pointed to a couch in the waiting area.

Looking around the room, I asked, "Does anyone else here have a port?"

One lady's hand shot up.

"Do you mind if I take a look?" I asked.

She showed me her port, and her skin looked normal without discoloration.

I looked back at the first lady and asked, "Is it warm if you touch it?"

"Yes," she said.

I walked over to her and told her that I felt it was an infection brewing. I said, "I am no doctor, but I think you should go to the hospital. It is right next door."

She said, "Well, my husband is tired, and he wants to go home."

I walked over to her husband to have a private conversation with him. "I know how challenging these past few months have been for your wife, but I also know how they have been for you. All eyes are on the cancer patient, and nobody thinks about the caregiver. I realize it has been emotionally draining for you. Your wife told me that you had been here all day, you live an hour away, and you are both tired."

He smiled, nodding in agreement, "Yes, we are."

I continued, "But I also know that your wife's port does not look good. While I am not a doctor, I know enough that an infection is present when the skin around a port turns pink or red. So I suggested to her that after class, you should stop at the E.R."

I know he wasn't happy hearing this because he let out a sigh and rolled his eyes.

I said, "The way I see it, you can drive an hour home and in the middle of the night when she wakes up with excruciating pain you will have to drive another hour to rush her back to the hospital... or you can stop when you leave here. Who knows, maybe I'm wrong. But if I'm right it will save you a trip."

Thankfully, he agreed, and when they left I gave them my cell number and asked them to please call and let me know how she was.

Sure enough, she called me later to tell me she had an infection. The doctors had immediately put her on intravenous antibiotics in hopes of getting ahead of it before it got worse.

Once again, I realized what listening to your intuition means. It's God, your guides, angels, or maybe Jesus speaking to you. Anyone can tap into their intuition. Those messages are there for a reason. While I am not perfect, I do my best to listen and act on them.

CHAPTER TEN

AIRLINE DAYS

I remember one day at work having a conversation with God in my mind. I asked if He would bring spiritual people to me. *If I have coworkers who think as I do, please have them cross my path.* I was tired of being in my own little world. None of my close friends thought as I did, and though they always listened intently and knew I wasn't making it up, they didn't really understand. I appreciated their support, but something was missing.

Shortly after that conversation I was working a flight with Christine. She had such a gentle way about her, a big smile and infectious laugh. She was also a musician who used to sing in clubs and play the piano. No wonder, I thought. She had a beautiful speaking voice and was also very spiritual. She practiced Reiki, which I knew nothing about at the time, and she gave the most incredible hugs that I felt to my core. It was as if God was holding you. I had only experienced that one other time in my life, and that was with my girlfriend Carol, who was a healer. If you have never experienced that, it is truly magical and something you will never forget.

I felt safe opening up with Christine as I knew she wouldn't judge me. She did, however, tell me to be careful who I shared these things with. Opening up was still new to me, and after she said that I retreated into myself once again. I worked with these people and I didn't want them to think I was off my rocker. It's pretty funny when I think about it, especially now that I am putting it all out there in a book!

When I look back, God had indeed sent me a handful of spiritual people to work with over the next couple of weeks. At the airline, you have a large group of coworkers who work flights. Each day you are assigned gates, and you never know who your partner will be for that one flight. Sometimes, you will work together on two flights, then move on to another gate and another person. The job is extremely high stress, so teamwork is vital. Some people are more open than others, but you can pick up who is on your wavelength if you listen. There were several of coworkers who were of like consciousness and I felt grounded knowing they were there. I met Ella, Yvette, Marti, Ann, Gabe, Tajie, and Ella's friend Anna. Anna was a beacon of hope for many as she battled with breast cancer. She taught me how to live and thrive when faced with adversity. Sadly, her time here was short, but she departed with a faith-filled heart and will always be remembered by those whose hearts she touched. I knew I could go to one of them if something was on my mind, especially when I intuitively knew I needed to view a situation through a different lens.

My mother was scheduled for surgery one day, but I had to work and was feeling terrible that I didn't fly to Seattle to be with her. I remember going through security, and when I gathered my items as they came through the scanner, I noticed a penny on the ground under the conveyor belt. I liked believing that it was my dad's way of letting me know he was there. So in my mind, I said to him, "No, Dad, I am not going to crawl underneath the belt to retrieve the penny today, but I appreciate your letting me know you are here and you're keeping an eye on Mom." I felt that was good enough, so I exited security and headed to Gate A18 to begin working an early morning flight to Chicago. I was the boarding agent, which meant I had to keep an eye on the door in case somebody tried to go down while also taking each ticket and eyeing carry-ons to make sure they would fit in the overhead. Early morning Chicago flights are always crazy!

One by one, the passengers came to hand me their tickets to scan. As I went to scan one gentleman's ticket, I looked at the name and said quite loud, "You've got to be kidding me!"

The poor passenger looked at me and said, "Excuse me?" as I started to cry.

My coworker came over, asking what was wrong and if she could help. Between my tears, I said, "This man's boarding pass says James Moore, my father's name. He passed years ago, but it just caught me off guard. I'm okay." I apologized to the passenger and handed him his ticket. In my tenure at the airline, I have easily boarded several million passengers and never once did any of them have my dad's name, but today, when mom was in surgery, I did.

The rest of the day was chaotic, but quitting time finally arrived. I clocked out and started walking up the ramp to exit the airport when right in front of me was a young sailor in full uniform. I nodded and thanked my dad for being there. My dad was in the Navy, and you rarely see sailors in uniform in Phoenix, especially exiting the airport. I knew again he was sending me a message that he had been looking after Mom. Her surgery was successful!

In 2013, my airline announced a pending merger with another, much larger airline, and the customer service agents at that airline were non-union. Having spent the vast majority of my career in union jobs, this was unacceptable to me. I got in touch with my local and told them we needed to dive in head-first! Thankfully, they had already been discussing it. They also knew what a strong union advocate I was as I had helped get the union in at our hometown airline before a previous merger.

In 2014, as per our contract, my union could pull me off work for union activity. My territory was west of the Mississippi, where I flew to the airports to speak to agents, hoping they would agree to sign union cards. I never once thought it would be a challenge, but it was because another union had been trying for twenty years to organize this workgroup. My personal feeling was they weren't with the number one union in the country! Looking back, I had always worked for number one. The number one newspaper in Seattle, the number one airline, and the number one union. Interesting.

While I am very personable and the majority of my coworkers liked me, I didn't know anyone at this other airline, so I had to tread carefully. I was intuitively guided to ask this one coworker, Scott, if he would be interested in joining me. We had only worked a couple of flights together, and he had come from the first merger, but I just had this *feeling* he was the one. I was right. Unlike me, Scott knew the contract forward and backward, and he managed my time when I would eagerly run off like a freight train or a dog hunting for a bone. I was excited to wake up every day. It reminded me how I felt as a child on Christmas morning. I was passionate about the campaign and making a difference. Many had never worked under a union contract, so it was up to us to explain everything, find out their concerns and turn those concerns into something positive that could potentially be included in our future contract. Scott was my go-to guy and, in hindsight, it was probably good to have a male with me as some would warm up more easily to a man.

He also kept me on track, reminded me to set my alarm, and told me where to be at what time. This was no easy feat, as procrastination and being tardy are things I've always struggled with. Scott and I were a great team, and it filled my heart immensely when we won the election that helped make a difference for so many.

On one of our flights, Scott wrote something on paper and handed it to me. To this day, it is on my wall in the office.

"What I desire is already here,

I just haven't connected to it yet.

I can't be stopped because my thoughts are aligned with the mind or intellect of God."

CHAPTER ELEVEN

THE AFTERLIFE CONFERENCE

In September 2015, AREI, the Afterlife and Research Education Institute, held a conference in Scottsdale. Having always been curious about where we're all eventually going, I jumped at the chance to purchase a ticket. The event was in a large hotel conference room, and they had break-out sessions with various well-known speakers so you could learn more about a topic that resonated with you.

There were two hundred participants in 2014; however, it had grown this year. Nearly four hundred people gathered to listen to the authors and scholars speak of the afterlife and afterlife communication. I was excited because Dick Sutphen would be there!

Dick Sutphen is the author of the *Master of Life Manual,* which, along with Louise Hay's *You Can Heal Your Life* was one of my first books on spirituality. He also wrote *Lighting the Light Within* and *You Were Born Again to Be Together,* among many others. I was so excited to meet Dick that I almost couldn't stand it! I know we aren't supposed to have idols, but he was the man who opened my eyes to the spiritual realm. I loved listening to him speak and signed up for his mailing list to stay connected. I was thrilled to learn that he was now living in Sedona and would be holding classes just ninety minutes away from me. It was like a dream come true!

That three-day conference was so incredible it inspired me to do a deeper dive spiritually. Erica was away at college, so it was just Bill and me at home. I still worked at the airline, but I needed to find something that interested me, and this did. It also helped to give me answers to questions I'd had for years but felt I couldn't discuss with just anybody.

I'd had numerous epiphanies throughout the weekend. First, I signed up for Sheri Perl's break-out session on Helping Parents Heal. One of my girlfriends had lost a son and was grieving. I wanted to know more about what Sheri offered before I recommended it to her. In the end, Sheri led us in a meditation, and it was pretty profound.

That morning, while driving to the seminar, I talked to my friend Kate, who had crossed over in 2009. She struggled with emphysema when she was alive, and we both knew she would go before me. I had made her promise to do everything within her power to visit, and she said she would. Now I was reminding her of that promise.

While in a meditative state it's easy for me to see visually, and that day I was even more deeply relaxed than usual. Sheri was guiding the group in an attempt for them to connect with their children across the veil. Since I didn't have a child on the other side, someone I loved would come through, but I was not even thinking about that; I was just listening and following along.

I saw a beautiful wooded setting with a river running through it. I was on one side of the river, and to my surprise, my friend Kate was on the other! I don't know how they do this, but she wore the patterned print dress I'd asked her husband for after she passed! In retrospect, I realize she wore an outfit I would remember and loved seeing her in. I find that notion amazing, and I guess I won't fully understand it until it's my time to go home. She looked beautiful and was smiling at me. It was our first contact since she died. I was surprised at our conversation.

"Kate! Why have you waited so long! I have been waiting!" I shouted at her. Yes, I was mad.

She graciously smiled and said, "You needed to go it alone, darling. I didn't want to be a crutch."

At that point, Sheri's meditation was concluding. I started crying, Kate disappeared, and I never got to thank her, ask questions, tell her I loved her or anything! I was so upset with myself for yelling at her after I had waited for so long. Then I felt terrible. I felt as if I had missed the moment. I tried not to let it consume me the rest of the day, but I couldn't help it.

Later that night, on the drive home, I knew all was well. I knew that Kate understood. As I am writing this, I find it interesting how I can *see* people in meditations. I was not touching anything of hers, I'd just been thinking of her earlier that morning, and there she was! As much as I would like to speak with her now, I know she knows it, just like I know I have to go it alone.

CHAPTER TWELVE

THE DIAGNOSIS THAT CHANGED EVERYTHING

I n 2016 I started taking classes at Southwest Institute of Healing Arts (SWIHA) in Tempe, AZ, to become a certified hypnotherapist. While I had no intention of using hypnotherapy to help people lose weight or quit smoking, I knew it gets you into a deeper state where mind over matter kicks in and you can conquer these things. The idea was to start with hypnotherapy, but the goal was to learn past life regression. The experience with Joy had changed my life, and I had a thirst for more knowledge. Why could I so easily see things? Could everyone if they tried?

Little did I know, as my classes at SWIHA were coming to an end in early 2017, I'd be faced with another health crisis, one in which self-hypnosis would come in handy.

It was February – President's Day, to be exact – when I had some lower abdominal pains after lunch. Assuming it was what I ate, I didn't think much of it; plus I knew I had a follow-up appointment with my general practitioner.

The next day I went to my doctor, and at the end of the appointment, she asked if there was anything else.

"Yes," I said. I've been having this stomach problem since yesterday, as I was rubbing below my belly.

"When was your last colonoscopy?" she asked.

Oh geez, I thought, *do we have to go there?* "Six years ago."

"Well, I want you to have a colonoscopy and an endoscopy. Here is the doctor I would like you to see," she said as she handed me a slip of paper.

"Lovely," I thought. *I don't want to do this, but the pain hasn't gone away.*

Later that day, I called to make an appointment. The receptionist said the doctor could see me in two months. Knowing I couldn't wait that long, I asked if there was someone else. She said, "Well, you can see the physician's assistant tomorrow morning."

"Great!"

By the time I saw this woman the following day, the pain had magically disappeared. Still, she said she wanted me to have a CT scan. Now I'm thinking, *The pain is gone. Is all this necessary?*

Thursday morning, I headed to the imaging place to have a CT. When I checked in, they told me the CT machine was down. I asked if there was another one in the Valley, and she said there was one in Gilbert, about thirty minutes from their office.

Off I went to Gilbert to have the CT. At four-thirty, as I was driving home on the freeway, my phone rang. It was the physician's assistant from the doctor's office, asking if I could come into the office because she already had my test results. I was shocked. I had just left the imaging place thirty minutes prior, and why would she want to see me?

Knowing they closed at five, I told her I was in Gilbert and wouldn't make it there in time. "You can just give me the results over the phone."

There was silence.

"Look, I've already survived breast cancer, I'm very spiritual, so I don't think anything you could say would shake me."

"Well, I don't usually like giving news like this on a Friday, so can you pull off the road?

"Sure," I said as I continued driving.

That's when I heard her voice as if it was in slow motion and suspended in time. "Mrs. Ewing, I am very sorry to tell you this, but you have liver cancer."

I said, "What? Wait a minute. Let me pull over."

Once I had pulled off the freeway as far as I could, I asked, "What are you talking about?"

"Well, you have lesions on your liver. We believe it is cancer. If you would like, I have already been texting an oncologist friend of mine, and he can see you on Monday. Would you like me to set that up for you?"

"Yes, please," I told her, "However, I think you're wrong. I know I don't have liver cancer."

My head was swirling as I drove home, but I didn't cry, which is strange because I am usually a very emotional person. When I got home, I told my husband, then I called Erica, then my mom and Dick. Everyone was in shock except me. I knew they were wrong. My family thought I was in denial. Bill couldn't even look at me.

"What's going on?" I asked. "Tell me! Look at me."

His eyes met mine, and he broke down. "I don't want to lose you!"

I looked at him, smiled, and said, "Well, I'm not going anywhere, so don't worry!"

Given how stoic I was, it's understandable why they would think I was in denial. I knew Jesus was with me, and I also knew there was a reason I had this. I had *seen* many years ago that I was going to live until at least age ninety-eight (now I say *ninety-eight or something greater!*), so I swear to God, I was not worried. I had no fear.

Bill, Erica, and I met with the oncologist on Monday, and he ordered a biopsy, which meant another CT scan. By March 9, we had the results. The doctor walked into the office and said, "Well, it's good news and bad news. The bad news is that it is cancer, but the good news is that it's neuroendocrine cancer. We will have to run more tests. It is stage 4 because it has spread, and we believe the primary is in your intestine because that is typical."

"Stage 4?" I thought. Well, I will keep that number to myself. I know my coworkers would probably freak out. I imagined whispering behind my back: "Did you hear Deb Ewing has stage 4 cancer?" In hindsight, I joke that I should've ridden that wave. Maybe coworkers would've rushed to pick up my work shifts to help me out!

I asked God what He wanted me to do with this diagnosis. He had answered me almost immediately when I had breast cancer, so I was surprised that He made me wait two months!

When the answer finally came, He said, "Help educate other doctors and nurses."

I already knew what He meant. At the time, there were only one hundred and twenty thousand people in the country who had been diagnosed with this.

Okay, so You want me to be a messenger again? Lovely.

I worked as long as I could, then I went on short-term disability. I also started going to a support group in Phoenix and was surprised to find that the people there knew more than my doctor! They were adamant that I cancel the colonoscopy and the dental implant surgery I had scheduled. They gave me the name of a neuroendocrine specialist in Arizona and told me to see him. I could no longer have epinephrine or Novocain; if I did I could go into cardiac arrest. Interesting that my oncologist didn't tell me that! I can't have any anesthesia without a Sandostatin drip. Huh? What's that? These two ladies in that group not only educated me, but I believe, saved my life!

The next six months were a whirlwind, but you know what surprised me most? My NET Specialist, the radiologist, and my surgeon in New Orleans (yeah, I had to fly to have surgery because no one in Arizona could operate on me at the time) all believed in their higher power. My surgeon even told me they prayed before surgery! I was divinely guided every step of the way, and I wasn't once fearful. When you have faith, there's no reason to be afraid.

I am sharing all of these things because I am supposed to. God wants me to create awareness about this disease because many people suffer for years with a misdiagnosis. The doctor tells the patient they have IBS, Crohn's disease, and the like. They didn't even teach it to students in medical school. Medical students were taught to look for something familiar rather than exotic causes for a disease. They are to expect common conditions, hence the phrase, "If you hear hoofbeats, think horses, not zebras." But like me, zebras do exist, and awareness is vital.

My general practitioner, who started me on this journey, congratulated me when she heard. "At least it won't kill you," she said. I was taken aback at that one and thought, *Tell that to the people in my support group who just died or the spouses who watched their partner die.* When I asked her how she knew to send me to this gastroenterologist, she smiled, pointed to the ceiling, and said, "I'm just glad I listened and didn't prescribe something like Prilosec for you." I appreciated that. Apparently, she gets *messages*, too.

Many in the neuroendocrine cancer community were upset when the media reported that Steve Jobs and Aretha Franklin died from pancreatic cancer. I am here to tell you they didn't. They had neuroendocrine cancer of the pancreas. Google it. The NET support forums wish they had been more forthcoming to raise awareness. Even still, some doctors will tell someone they are inoperable. It's because many times they don't know what to do! There have been times when I read a post in our Facebook community, and if I am spiritually guided, I personally reach out to them. I know two people that I was in contact with who got surgery. I told them my doctor's name and to not give up. One was a lady checking in beside me at my surgeon's office in New Orleans. She reached over, tapped me on the arm, and said, "Excuse me, are you, Debra Ewing?"

I looked at her, surprised because, after all, I was in Louisiana. She introduced herself, and I immediately hugged her. That's when I heard a voice behind me saying, "Is she the reason we are here?" I turned around, and it was her mother! Her doctor had said she was inoperable, and there wasn't much hope. I intuitively knew they were wrong, and my surgeon was able to give her a couple more years of her life, long enough to see her beautiful grandson born. Another young man, the father of three small boys, had surgery and is still alive. I'm sure God is guiding me. There is no doubt. It's just amazing to me how many doctors don't know what they don't know!

I ended up taking a year off to heal before returning to work; however, that was still too much for me. The monthly injection I will receive for the rest of my life slays me energetically, among other side effects that I have been able to semi-manage. I worked full-time but benefited from a flexible schedule to drop, swap, and pick up shifts. Luckily for me, a part-timer wanted full-time hours, so we just swapped shifts. As it was, five hours a day was still too much, and I was even dropping shifts toward the end of that first year back. Every morning when I went into work, I would have a quiet conversation with God after getting through the TSA security checkpoint.

"Please put me where I can be of the best service to others today," I'd say as I looked down the packed concourse before me and saw hundreds of bobbing heads. I honestly tried, but after one year, it was just too much. While home, I spent my days on the couch, and it was not living. I was utterly exhausted. Thank God I learned early on from the more senior ladies at the Seattle Times to always take disability insurance if your employer offered it. You don't ever want to worry about finances when faced with a life-altering health issue.

Once I regained my energy, or should I say, started adapting to my *new normal*, which was a far cry from the Energizer Bunny I used to be, I started looking at online spiritual classes I could take from home on my own timeline. Not one to sit idle and just watch television all day or read books, I like learning about things that interested me and of course the afterlife was one of them.

CHAPTER THIRTEEN

ELECTRONIC VOICE PHENOMENON

I t was time for a spiritual respite! The previous months had drained me, and I was excited that AREI had another conference in Scottsdale. Once again, the speaker guest list was a who's who in spiritual circles, and in addition to appearing at these kinds of events they offered online classes, held events of their own, and were published authors. They all had one thing in common: to be of service to others. I had been mesmerized when I attended my first conference, and now I wanted to learn more about death and dying and possibly learn how to connect with loved ones across the veil.

I was glad to see my friend Mary there because I knew how desperately she wanted to connect with her son David. It was also good for grounding me. It always helps to be surrounded by people whose focus and energy matches mine spiritually.

I was surprised when Mary rushed over to me with her laptop, saying, "Debra, you've got to listen to this!"

We walked over to a bench and sat down. Mary had a session with Sheri Perl, from *Helping Parents Heal*, who does Electronic Voice

Phenomenon. EVP is a technology they have been experimenting with and perfecting for quite some time. In this session, Mary asked David if he was there. His response was only something Mary would recognize.

"Yes, Woman," came the voice through the machine. Nobody knew that "Woman" was a nickname for his mother, so there was no making that up!

It was brief and garbled with static, like a transistor radio that's not entirely dialed to the correct channel. Still, it was audible, especially to a mother desiring to know more.

Attempts began in the 1940s using technology to communicate with the deceased and have progressed in the years since. Still, when I'd first heard of the *SoulPhone®*, I wasn't sure if I was ready to sit in on a class. I mean, talk to the dead? Come on. How can that be possible? Then in came Mary and her son in spirit to change my perspective completely.

Dr. Gary Schwartz, a University of Arizona professor who earned his Ph.D. at Harvard, developed an interest in afterlife communication while working as a professor at Yale and is considered by many as an expert in this field. He is the Director of Laboratory for Advances in Consciousness & Health and heads up the project. If someone of his caliber is doing this, it can't be that far off or crazy, I thought, so I became a member of the SoulPhone Foundation to be on their email list and receive updates on the technology. I know, I know. If you think it's right up there with UFOs, I don't blame you, but then who thought I'd be talking to Jesus? I am laughing as I write this because by now you probably think I need to see a psychiatrist.

They have also created other devices, including the SoulSwitch™, SoulVideo™, and more. SoulVideo will also enable webinars with esteemed deceased luminaries who are working on ways to improve what they were doing while living on earth. As Nikola Tesla said during one meeting: *If you think what I was inventing while on earth was amazing, wait until you see what I've been working on here!*

Dr. Mark Pitstick is the Director of the SoulPhone Foundation and assists Dr. Schwartz in his research. He has forty-seven years of experience and training in hospitals, pastoral counseling settings, mental health, and holistic wellness clinics. After working in hospitals with many suffering and dying adults and children, he was motivated to find sensible, evidence-based answers to people's tough questions.

Both gentlemen have written several books and have had various TV interviews and documentaries. Please check their websites in the References section at the back of the book.

Does it sound too far out? No, not really when you consider that cell phones, vehicles that don't require gasoline, and self-driving cars are already here. They are, technologically speaking, just the tip of the iceberg!

In my research, I learned that one of Thomas Edison's least-known inventions was the Spirit Phone. However, his former associate, and bitter rival, Nikola Tesla, was also developing a similar mysterious device at the same time. The book *Edison vs. Tesla: The Battle Over Their Last Invention* examines their quest to talk to the dead.

Still skeptical? All I am asking is for you to consider, "What if…?"

Running into Mary started my day off on a high note, and I knew this was just the beginning!

I was also immediately drawn to hear what Suzanne Giesemann, another guest at the conference, had to say. Just from her professional attire, she exuded a level of credibility and confidence that stood out among others. I intuitively knew I needed to make changes to my speaker schedule so I wouldn't miss her. Suzanne, an evidential medium, captured me the minute she began to speak. She said she was there to share her story and give hope to those who had doubts.

Describing herself as an "unlikely medium," Suzanne recounted her story as a commanding officer in the U.S. Navy and an aide to the Chairman of the Joint Chiefs of Staff. Witnessing the ravages of the 9/11 attacks firsthand made her realize how short life can be, so she retired from the military and she and her husband sold their home and purchased a forty-six-foot sailboat. They were living out their dream of sailing around the world until they received an email with instructions to call home at the next port. The email didn't seem urgent, so they had no idea that call would change their lives forever. Suzanne's stepdaughter, Susan, who was pregnant at the time and a sergeant in the military, had been struck by lightning and died.

Overcome with grief and looking for answers, Suzanne remembered a book she had once read about mediumship. She made an appointment for herself and her husband with a medium, and they found their dear daughter was waiting from across the veil to talk to them. Suzanne shares her entire journey in a fantastic book called *Messages of Hope, The Metaphysical Memoir of a Most Unexpected Medium.*

After hearing her at the conference, I started following her, read her book, and have even taken some of her classes. She is a powerful yet loving woman and, indeed, the last person you'd think would become a medium. According to her, she does not possess any special "gifts," just innate human abilities that anyone can access if they will only trust the process.

CHAPTER FOURTEEN

I HEARD JESUS

Fast forward to what was hopefully nearing the end of the COVID-19 pandemic, when an author and publisher named Kim Richardson came across my screen. As I'm a strong believer that there are no accidents (and we shared many mutual friends on Facebook), I decided to look at what she was offering.

It turned out Kim was looking for sixty female aspiring authors to contribute to a book called *365 Days of Self-Love*. Each would write six chapters, four hundred words apiece, sharing their knowledge of honoring and loving the self. The idea was that every day for an entire year the reader would read one page on which to reflect and, hopefully, take action. I found this very interesting and felt it had come at the perfect time to get me out of my comfort zone and take a leap of faith in becoming a published author. After speaking with Kim, I got on board and got writing. It was a wonderful project – I learned a lot and was honored to be part of a terrific group of women, but more importantly, I now believed I could write my own book!

As I stated earlier, I'd known for years that I was supposed to write a book – I just didn't think it was this one! I want you to know that I didn't write this book alone. I was divinely guided; it came *through* me. To those of you unfamiliar with automatic writing, it is a process where you go into a meditative or trance-like state, then put the pen to paper and see what happens. I used to start by drawing circles over and over and over again while praying. At some point your subconscious mind starts to take over, and you won't remember what you wrote until you read it later. I have also typed the same sentence over and over, and the same thing happens – the typing takes on a mind of its own. That is how I finished writing this book. I could never have anticipated what transpired.

On a visit to Sedona several years ago, I hiked out to Bell Rock, home of one of the many magical energy vortexes in the area. I sat down with a pen and paper and just started scribbling circles, over and over and over again in the hopes that my pen would take over, though I was a little nervous about what or who would come through. Well, it could not have been better! It was my dad! I was shocked that he told me to let go of the hammer, which was the only thing of my father's that I wanted after he passed. His hands had used that hammer to build houses, and Bill gave it to the workmen to use one day, and it disappeared. I was so angry. I know Bill didn't mean for that to happen but unfortunately, I chose to grind around in it for several years.

Automatic writing is a wonderful experience, and I have used this method several times since to communicate with him. Again, when I am in this deep state I have no idea what I am writing; they are not my words so it's always a shock to see them afterward. What Dad said gave me peace of mind. He also shared something about heaven. Of course there was no way of verifying this, so I just filed it away, knowing that someday I would find out for myself.

It all became apparent in the wee morning hours of January 2021, when Jesus came to me and told me to write the book. I immediately responded, "Okay," though I had no idea how it would transpire or how I would pay for it. I just trusted He would show me the way, just as I trusted Him when I signed my publisher's contract. My life would be forever changed.

To my surprise, once that happened, it was as if the Universe or God opened the doors, and everything started falling into place. The classes that presented themselves, the teachers, the virtual writing retreats – each step came in perfect sequence, building upon the one before it. It was as if I was starting at the bottom of a staircase, and with each step I took I got closer to the goal. If my conscious mind started being concerned about money and how I would pay for all of this, I stopped, put it in check, and released it to the Universe. I just *knew* that God would provide a way, though of course I was curious and a little bit anxious about how this would transpire! Once again it reminded me of being a child on Christmas morning and noticing a big package underneath the tree. How filled with anticipation I'd be to find out what was inside! That's the same feeling I get when I think about this book reaching the masses. I am reminded, *all is well,* and *Thy will be done,* and to *trust the process.*

CHAPTER FIFTEEN

WRITING RETREATS

There is a saying that when the student is ready, the teacher will come, and in my case, that's exactly what happened with Tom Bird.

In 2019, I signed up for one of his live retreats in Sedona that was scheduled for March of the following year. That's my birthday month and this three-day getaway was my gift to myself. Then COVID-19 hit; restaurants and businesses closed, and seminars were postponed indefinitely! I was so disappointed, but thinking everything happens for a reason, I chose to let it go. I knew this pandemic couldn't go on forever, could it?

In the meantime, Tom offered virtual courses. Virtual? No, that's not for me. I wanted to be in Sedona to do this, so I ignored the offers to sign up until one of my teachers, Colette Baron-Reid, said something that turned a light on inside me:

"Just because you want to manifest a house with a brown picket fence, don't overlook a home just because the fence is white."

That made sense, and I realized it was precisely what I had been doing with those emails about the virtual seminar. I signed up, and since then I have learned not to be stuck on how I think things should be. It might arrive in a completely different package!

I knew I was supposed to do prep work before my writing class, and at best, I was a poor student; plus, I was busy helping to plan Erica's wedding, which had also been postponed one year due to covid. I had no idea what to expect from the class, but I went in with the goal of finishing the book I had started in 1987. As I would soon learn, God had a different plan.

Intuitively I knew I was supposed to write about my experience with Jesus as a teen, but I knew I had this other book still sitting there. Again, you don't always get what you think you should or what you ask for. This is how this book unfolded and how an unexpected friendship came to be. This was beyond my wildest imagination. All I wanted was to give people the same hope I have found, which made it easier for me to live with a dis-ease the doctors can't seem to cure. I also thought I would be writing this book on my own.

When the pre-retreat webinar commenced, Tom started with open ended questions by saying, "I am grateful for …" He repeated this over and over, and we were to write as he instructed. Yes, it seemed redundant, but I trusted this process; after all, Tom is the expert and I was there to learn from him so I would get the most value from the upcoming weekend retreat. He gave me a method to follow, and like the circles I would draw over and over in an automatic writing process, I was shocked when I repeatedly typed as he instructed and the answers were flying from my fingers on the keyboard.

CHAPTER SIXTEEN

UNEXPECTED CONVERSATIONS

Thursday, February 18, 2021

I had been waiting with great anticipation for the in-person retreat, but a year later we were still in pandemic mode. However, once again, Spirit knocked on my door with another way, and this time I paid attention!

The retreat was held via Zoom and started with the *Divine Author Within* (DAW) music playing in the background, as the rhythm made it easier to connect with Spirit. Next, we recited the Author's Prayer three times before starting to enter a meditation-like consciousness. Being a certified hypnotherapist, I was used to tuning in.

"Stand up, stand up!" Tom said sternly to get our attention. "Take a deep breath in and exhale fast, take a deep breath in, and *exhale*, ahhhhh. Let it all go. . . Breathe normally, open your eyes. Now, we're going to start writing. Let your words lead the way, let your heart lead the way."

He paused, then asked, "What are you thankful for?" Another pause. "Keep typing. What are you thankful for?"

I began to type.

"I am thankful for Bill."

"I am thankful for Erica."

"I am thankful for my monthly injection."

"I am thankful for life."

"I am thankful my mom is here with me and that she has Dick in her life."

"I am thankful for my doctor who can keep me alive."

"I am thankful for my breath."

"I am thankful for Jesus and my relationship with him. I know that He is with me."

"I am thankful that my father can come through as he did on Erica's wedding day to let me know he would be with us."

"I am thankful to Tom Bird for this opportunity to connect with Spirit and continue writing," and, "I am thankful to be here."

My thoughts were running rampant at this point, while my fingers struggled to keep up. *Please tell me what direction I am supposed to go in. I know you are with me. I know you will guide me. This time with you is very sacred to me. Come on in. Let's have a chat. I am waiting for you.*

I continued, *Hey, aren't you proud of how I moved through the family wedding drama? Come on. I have grown, haven't I? I know you know. It's been a very stressful week.*

Thank you for getting me through it while keeping my head above water! For God's sake, oops, excuse me. You know what I mean, though, don't you? Talk to me, please. I want to feel you. I know you are there.

Tom interrupted. "Who am I, why was I born, and what was I born to do?"

Trying to be patient, I said to myself. "I am a child of God. I was born to return to complete the lessons I haven't finished. I was born to talk about my relationship with Jesus. I am here to share, to be open, to comfort others, and release their fears. I am to help ease pain and teach about the other side, the side across the veil so that others won't have fear."

I started smiling then, because I could feel His presence.

Finally, He said, *People trust you. They believe in you. I can share my word through you, My dear. I need you to bring comfort only you are the vehicle I am using. You are likable.*

People will listen.

"But how am I supposed to do that?" I asked.

By writing the book, dear Debra. Write the book. Share your experiences with me, all of them, even if they sound crazy to you. Remember, dear one, Trust the Process. That is all you have to do. Trust the process; the answers will come. Keep spending time with me. Go out in nature. It is sometimes easier to reconnect that way. Don't you love your backyard? It is beautiful, and the mornings are so peaceful. I know it calms you. Talk with me there. Go for a walk in your neighborhood. I will be there with you. And Debra, please, after you finish this book, you must work on the one to help empower women! You cannot waste any more time on that one. You must complete it. You have many things to do. You must set a clear path to accomplish them. Get a chart or a planner. Carve out your day the night before. It truly is an excellent habit to get into, that way you aren't flying blind, and you accomplish so much more.

Wouldn't that be wonderful?

"Yes, it would. I would feel better about myself as well!"

Of course you would, so do it, dear.

Tom said, "Close your eyes, see God and ask, 'How do I know you're God?'"

I heard Him laugh. *Well, who else would I be?*

"I don't know if you are God or Jesus."

Well, God is within you. It's the very essence of your being. You know I am Jesus because I have been with you all of your life.

"Yeah, I know that. And I trust you. I mean, who wouldn't trust you!"

Debra dear, you have already lived two-thirds of your life. You do not have time to waste. Please make this a priority. As of now, there is nothing more important than our work. Don't let the outside influences sway or distract you. You've got this. You've got a gift.

You've got a message to share.

"Will I be able to get messages from people across the veil this time when I take Suzanne's class? Oh. I am sorry. That is a ridiculous question. I already know the answer. If I can bring people in now, why wouldn't I? I need to trust myself, don't I?"

Yes, dear, you do. You already have the gift. Why not say a prayer beforehand and ask for support and guidance from your angels and your guides. It may make you relax so they can come. Would you please try that?

Tom asked, "God, what is there that I need to forgive myself for? Would you please tell me now?"

You need to forgive yourself for talking sharply with your mother when you were young. You have already made that shift, so let it go.

You need to forgive yourself for having sex. You were looking for love when all you really had to do was look inside and love yourself.

You need to forgive yourself for shaming your body. Debra, please, love your body, love the body I gave you. Hasn't it carried you through two health crises? There is so much more than sex. I don't know why you held that in such high regard or allowed it to define you.

That is absurd. You are more than that, My dear!

You need to forgive yourself for spending money and getting into debt. Doesn't the Universe always provide exactly what you need? It's okay, dear. Let it go.

You need to forgive yourself for teaching your daughter to drive fast. She has already learned that lesson.

"What intention would be best for me to focus on in my life right now, and what would taking action on that realistically look like?" Tom asked.

I was laughing now, because Jesus and I had already covered that.

Set a goal first, though, Debra. We did not discuss that. Set a goal with a deadline. A deadline, dear one, will put a fire under you to complete the work! Get with your studies!

Somebody may need a minister unexpectedly, and you could be standing by to fill in. We have already discussed the books. The first one will give you a presence. The rest will follow. Look at that young man you helped today. Didn't it feel good helping him? Next, look at life coaching. You already have that gift. However, it never hurts to learn new tools to put in your toolbox. Learn about business or have someone else do it for you. I know you have fatigue and feel limited; however, you can start the groundwork, lay out a plan, and start! It will make you feel so much better to have a plan. Maybe you should schedule regular sessions with me? Think about it. I am here. All you have to do is ask!

"Thank you for showing me the way. Thank you for giving me a goal. Thank you for bringing Tom Bird into my life! Being able to converse with you is unbelievably great!!"

Debra, don't put off strength training. I know you have gotten out of the habit since this health journey, but please get started. I will be there to support you, and you will feel so much better.

Tom asked, "How and when will we next meet?"

Jesus laughed as He said, *You know that all you have to do is ask for me, and I will be there." You see, these questions are for people who don't already have a relationship with me, but you and I, we go way back, in this lifetime, fifty-two years, Debra. Sometimes I will automatically appear even when you don't know that you need me! I know you have no concern about that.*

DAY ONE
Reflections

When I reflected on yesterday, it almost seems impossible that what happened truly did. Who is ever going to believe me?

I watched *Conversations With God* for a second time last night, hoping it would give me a better understanding of what Neale Donald Walsch experienced to see if I could glean anything from watching it. People believed him right away. Will people believe me? I guess that is my thinking brain getting in the way of my spiritual flow, and I should not concern myself with the *what-ifs* and just go with the flow. I laugh as I write it because that was said to me several days ago. *Go with the flow, Deb.* If you fight it, you are wasting time. Just sink into it and go with the flow. Ah, yes, as I look at the picture of Jesus on my desk with his arms outstretched, I can see in my memory from yesterday His smile. That is it. I have got it. Just do it. Publish the book, and all will be well.

In hindsight, I should have asked him other questions, including some about the various religions and those who identify as agnostic. In my thinking brain, I believe that we are all on a path to get to the same goal: enlightenment. Be it Christianity, Judaism or Islam – each faith has similar components, including the existence of one God. Other belief systems also acknowledge God or gods, though It/They may be different than what Christians, Jews and Muslims believe in, while others do not believe in any deity.

I used to think that God was this almighty being with long white hair and a long white beard sitting in a chair. I remember as a child seeing someone that I thought depicted Him in a show like the Little Mermaid and believed he was an underwater God. Now I cannot see a face for God; instead, I imagine God as a type of being, energy, consciousness, and I feel that God or God-like power is in every one of us. That is why I have such a hard time with all of the hatred in the world, and in particular the current political landscape in the United States. There is no honor. Respect is missing. There is too much anger. There is no love. It is pitting friends – and even worse, family members – against each other. The news has never been so toxic, and it makes me so sad that I need to shut it off for my well-being.

Why can't people go within to release it, or do they just not want to? Maybe they are not aware and do not know how? Maybe I need to go within again, and the answers will come, or He will speak to me with guidance. I know I have the ability to effect change. I have done it before, and it is such a wonderful love-based feeling that fills my body with this swirling vortex of vibrating love. It is hard to put it into words, but it is the best feeling when I am in this space, and I genuinely want that for our world. I want everyone to experience this all-encompassing feeling and way of being.

DAY TWO

Friday, February 19, 2021

I had such an incredible day yesterday with Jesus. It was almost so magical that I wanted to keep it to myself. It is so hard to explain. I tried to tell my husband last night, but understandably it was a little much for him. I hope others will be open, and then I hear *trust the process,* and I am at peace.

I can't describe this God-like feeling that comes over me when I am in this space. The tears just come, and I feel so peaceful. I am one with the source. I am one with God. And it is magical. Last night, while watching the *Conversations with God* movie, I gained some insight, but I know I need to read his books. I laugh as I write this because I don't enjoy reading that much, yet I have hundreds of spiritual books on my shelves. I know He will guide me. I also feel like it is too much to ask Him back today, but of course that is silly. He said He would be there for me any time I asked. Why does it make me feel that I am selfish? Maybe unworthiness to be in His presence? I mean, who am I to experience this gift? It is unimaginable. I realize that, but it has happened to me. To my conscious mind my visions and interactions do not seem plausible, until I remember that Pauline saw Him. That was a second validation for me. These are gifts I cannot explain, but someday I hope to.

I wish I had an answer for peace on the planet, but I feel I can only create it in my own circle. Ahh yes. My circle, but like a pebble dropped into a body of water, it has a ripple effect. I am laughing as I visualize this. A ripple effect. That is what my book will have. That is what it will hopefully do for others. I do not have to concern myself as to whether people will believe it. I just need to release it because, after all, it did happen to me. It is my life story. And that is all that matters.

I never thought that this book could segue into my recovery book for women. Wow. Now that is a concept. I can actually imagine virtual classes, starting with a meditation, then the lesson, and finishing up with relaxing music where the participants write about the feelings that come up and hopefully shift into automatic writing. I believe it's important to connect with God, write and release, know that God is with them and willing to share thoughts and ideas that will produce an epiphany to move faster through the mire. That is beautiful! But how do I accomplish that, and how will I have the energy?

Jesus said one step at a time. One step. Each one builds on the other. Take the first step and then ask Him to come in again. Don't think about the future. Stay in the present. *Focus,* He said, and I remember laughing. He must know that's sometimes hard for me to do. My husband laughs when I am in the kitchen making something, I leave the room and then come back for Windex and paper towels. I laugh in reflection. What does cleaning the mirror in the bathroom have to do with what I was doing in the kitchen? Yes, I need to focus. The rest will reveal itself when it is time.

Be patient, dear one.

Wow. He is here again. He is off to my left, watching me as I write this. It is so overwhelming being in His presence that tears just start flowing.

My conscious mind kicks in…who do I think I am to spread the word of Jesus like this? Well, it's not really His word. It is my story, with, well, yes, His word. Then I am reminded of Tom's prayer: *Thank you for leading me to surrender any fears, doubts, worries, and concerns that have stood in the way of me experiencing the oneness we share.* That needs to be my mantra. I haven't seen Jesus in such a long time that it's incredible to think I can call on Him.

Meditate. Yes, yes, I laugh as I remember. Didn't He tell me yesterday that He was sending me messages? I need a new ritual. I need to schedule it. Once I have the routine, it will be our time. *Our time.* I can see it now. But I need to stay in the present. Everything will unfold as it is supposed to. I am not one to just sit idle. I have been waiting for Him to tell me. I have been waiting for Him to guide me. However, I thought it would be coming from God, not Jesus, but sometimes I feel as if it is God. Maybe it is God speaking through Jesus? We have the vibration of God inside us. Sometimes I get confused about who is speaking to me, and yesterday I went back and corrected some of the writing because it sounded like God, but Jesus was speaking to me.

Jesus didn't create the earth, yet I typed *When I created earth or the planet*. Knowing that Jesus didn't, I changed it. I guess I shouldn't get caught up in the details. I should just type what He says. So many times, we got caught up in the intricacies of things. Like my friend Laura does with her resume. I am laughing as I reflect on our conversation regarding it. Just get the damn thing out! It does not have to be perfect, for God's sake! There I go again, using His name. Hmmm, I wonder where that phrase came from?

Just let it flow, Deb. Let it flow. You have had so many experiences that you can share to help women live better lives. You started that book so many years ago, and now it is time to let it flow. It's something you must do. You have a gift to share with others. Get it out there. Do not be afraid.

Dear one, do not be afraid. I am with you. I will guide you. Remember I told you that all you have to do is call on me and I will be there. I will help you. Do you not think it hurts Me to see others suffering?

As I hear and write this, I shake my head. He comes easily. He's back again. He heard me through my mind. I did not verbally ask for Him, yet here He is. Remember, do not get caught up in the system or how it will work.

I will show you when the time is right. One book at a time. Remember when you got on the stage and spoke in front of a group of Teamster women?

"Yes," I laughed.

You were scared, weren't you?

"Yes."

But you believed in what you were doing. It was your passion. Passion erases fear.

As I am listening, I shake my head in amazement. I would never have remembered that! I find it so interesting how He can reel me right back into memories from my life and remind me to experience the feeling over again. The *feeling*. It is what it's all about, just like in Jay Shetty's *Five-Day Habit Reset*. It was about the *feeling*. The book on clutter. It is about the *feeling*. Maybe it is the *feeling* and remembrance of it that helps one to move forward.

"Thank you for reminding me of that feeling. I had forgotten. I was in my element."

Of course, you were, He said, *and you will be in your element again once this book is out, and then the next. The first time you visually connect with women online, your heart will race and then skip a beat, but remember that I am with you. When you get stuck, I will be there as your voice to remind you. You will not fail, dear one. You will succeed in helping countless women, so you must do it. You are no longer that young lady you once were; however, your wisdom has multiplied, making you even more inspirational. I know you have touched many by how you handled your current health issue. You have inspired them. Trust the process, My dear. Trust the process.*

I could sense Him smiling then.

Remember?

Now that is love.

I opened my eyes and reached for my glass of water. Then I remembered I'd heard a message come in on my cell phone. When I saw who it was, I excitedly returned to typing.

"Oh my God. You sent her, didn't You? Okay. Thank You. I just get so emotional when I am with You. Alena. How could I forget Alena? We lost touch over the holidays. I am laughing as I write this. Yes, Alena. Of course. She is my girl. We have talked about doing this work together. There are no accidents! Now that is amazing! I am laughing just thinking about it. My God, You certainly have a sense of humor! Wow! Today is such an emotion-packed morning for me. Yesterday was emotional enough, but I feel each day will build, and of course, tomorrow is Saturday, so chances are You will be here, too, right? I almost feel like You are my new friend. I know that may sound crazy, but when one is divinely guided, there just are no words. You are using me to share. People trust me. Yet again, I wonder, why me? And then I remember You saying yesterday, *Why not you?*"

Trust the process, My dear. Trust the process. I am here.

DAY THREE

Saturday, February 20, 2021

"Talk to God," Tom reminded us. "Listen to God."

"Speak to me, tell me what I am supposed to write? What am I supposed to know?" I asked.

Finish the book, came that now very familiar voice. *Finish the book. I know you think the book called Recovered is supposed to be from you. Some of it is, but I will direct you through the rest of it. You cannot write it alone. Sure, you have some essential aspects of it, but there is more. So much more. They need to connect on a God level so they don't feel as if they are alone. I will give you answers. Are there any questions you want to ask of Me now that I might be able to help with the completion of the first book?*

"Yes, how do you feel about agnostics? Can you help me with that one?"

He laughed. *That is an interesting one. You see, they have not experienced My presence yet. They are caught up in the dogma of what churches preach and what they may have read in the Bible. Did God take a rib from Adam to create Eve? I have no way of proving that to you. You either believe it, or you don't, but ask yourself, what if?*

"Jesus, what do You want me to know about myself?"

I want you to know how grateful I am that you open yourself up. Take the time over these days to connect with Me. You see, I am always here, yet you don't take the time. Dear one, if you start your mornings with Me, your days will be better beyond measure. You connect and surrender; let Me guide you. I will guide you in all aspects of your life. Your health, well-being, your daily routine, your workouts, and your writing. Do not stop when the weekend is over. It would help if you poured it from you. I will show you the way. Just trust that. I am always here. Trust the process, remember? He smiled.

Thank you, God/Jesus, for being here with me. I cannot convey how much I appreciate this connection I have. It is so magical and sacred. There is no way I can explain it to anyone, but I feel so loved, nurtured, and comforted knowing You are with me on this path. Sometimes my mind starts to doubt... Is this truly real? How can it be? It is so simple, yet as I sit here in silence today, I know it is You and that You are here. And I am grateful that life is so good. I now know I will commit to my studies. I want to learn more. It will only deepen our connection. If everyone could experience this, wouldn't the world be such a better place? When I struggle, I will read my writing prayer to erase any doubt that might creep in. I know You are there. Life is good. Life is great! I am so glad I decided to take this course now. Thank you, God. I was ready. And I am ready. I surrender and am willing to have You show me the way.

CHAPTER SEVENTEEN

"KEEP WRITING"

Sunday, February 21, 2021

This morning in meditation, I asked Jesus what the next step was.

Keep writing, He said. *That is the vehicle to reach people.*

"Alright. I can be at peace with that."

"This three-day writing retreat forced you to focus and make the commitment to your writing that you started many years ago. Remember, I told you earlier that you must focus and trust the process. When you commit, you can move mountains."

Then He added, *Haven't you already seen that with your husband Bill? Look at what he did in regards to his health. I have never seen a mere mortal so committed. Once he started, he couldn't stop. I know that he was unhappy before, but look at how he won this time around! He needs to learn there are no failures. They are only lessons. Please try to get that point across. I do not want people to think they are failures. It reminds Me of watching someone take their hand and make it in the shape of an L and place it across their forehead.* He shakes his head. *Why on earth would you do that to yourself? Why would you make that your self-fulfilling prophecy? People need to empower themselves. If you are in emotional turmoil, find a teacher to help build you back up. My dear, look at what you have done! You didn't stop learning and growing, and now you share yourself to help others. That is what life is all about – paying it forward. It is so simple. Why don't others see it?*

"I can't tell You how much I love my time with You," I confided. "I wish others would be willing to try it."

They can if they believe and go within. I will come. If doubts or fears arise, they need to put those aside. If I could talk to all people, your world would be a much better place to live. You are wise to detach from the political landscape. There will only be more strife. I do not know how to eradicate it. What did you think when you saw Marianne Williamson attempting to run for presidential office?

"I was stunned," I replied, a bit surprised by His question. "I thought, how can Marianne Williamson be running? She has no political background."

Think about it, dear one. It was a way for Me to move consciousness to another dimension, that is all. It was a way to bring some level of peace. People opened their eyes by putting her in that arena. Follow her. Read about her. He laughed. *Well, I know you don't typically read books, but see what she is all about. Listen to some of her talks. Let Me know what you think.*

Now it was my turn to laugh. "You want ME to let YOU know what I think about Marianne Williamson?"

Yes. Does that seem odd?

"Of course, it does!" I placed my hands over my face and shook my head in disbelief. "I am having a hard time believing I'm even conversing with You! Some of the things You say or ask are from some other consciousness. I can't think this stuff up. I hope other people realize it."

Just remember, some will, some won't…nexxxt! Isn't that what you read somewhere? He said, laughing.

"Yes, but coming from *You?*" I asked. "Even when I go back to proofread what I wrote, I am blown away because I don't remember writing that! And it's like You magically shift in, and the words start coming again, even during editing! It is almost like I feel I am in some type of a dream or, I don't know, maybe it's like what tripping on some illegal drug must be. I apologize. I don't mean to reference our connection that way, but I have no other way to explain it! I am speechless, and it takes a lot for that to happen!"

He laughed again. *I know that dear. But, remember, I know everything.* Then His tone grew more serious. *You have gifts, dear one. Trust the process. You let fear get in the way, and that slows you down. If you meditate regularly, it will erase any fear and doubt, okay?*

That three-day weekend was sacred, and marked a turning point in my relationship with Jesus. It was more magical than anything I had ever experienced. Though I can recount these exchanges to you, there are no words to explain the feeling of unconditional love that accompanied them. He is my best friend. He is someone I can go within and share everything with, and He will tell me what I need to know. When I look back at what I wrote, I see the many typos I left as my fingers danced across the keyboard, trying to keep up with all He was saying. Yet the message comes through loud and clear.

I want everyone who is reading this to be able to experience it. Even if you never thought about writing a book or anything else, I encourage you to at least try, for this is something entirely different. I heard about automatic writing in the late 1980s, but I had a different mindset, and to be honest, I was afraid. You may think, *Well, she sees dead people, or she gets messages, so it is only natural for her to be able to do this.* However, I want to tell you, you can too. At the back of the book is a link to receive instructions for an easy way to connect with your loved ones. I believe we all have the ability. All you have to do is believe that it can happen and trust the process.

CHAPTER EIGHTEEN

FORGIVENESS & LIFE

Thursday, May 6, 2021

While in a deep meditative state we did a process about forgiveness, and I was amazed at what came up in my writing. Because it involves sensitive information about my family and had nothing to do with my connection with Jesus, I have chosen to omit it from the book. However, I will share what He told me about forgiveness. When you cannot forgive someone, it can eat away at your soul like a cancer that robs you of living your best life.

Forgiving someone is challenging, but it doesn't have to be. When you forgive someone, you give up the hope of how you thought things would or should be, thus setting yourself free.

During the pandemic, I'd had a few tumultuous months over family situations. When I was in this state, the things that came through the keyboard surprised me and gave me a different perspective. I realized the best course of action for me was to step back and let things unfold naturally. All one can do is be the best and most authentic version of themselves while also sending love to others. When you send love, it releases the resentment inside you, and maybe someday you will feel the love in return.

Conflict with others is painful, especially when it involves family, but I believe everything happens for a reason and try to look deeper. Sometimes my attempts are unsuccessful, especially when my emotions are involved, but now I try to take them out of the equation. I have learned through my studies that when one has an emotional response to something, they are not utilizing their higher God-mind but are under the influence of their ego or what someone may have told them. However, when they take a step back and go within, they can see there might be a bigger picture.

Also, until we are standing in someone else's shoes, we don't really know what is going on, and possibly they haven't recognized it in themselves yet. It's not our job to point it out. Divine timing takes care of the lessons, and while we are waiting for that to unfold, there is also a lesson for ourselves if we pay attention and recognize it.

My dad used to say, "You can forgive, but you don't forget." I believe he said that when someone was untrustworthy. When a person breaks your trust, it is painful – for you and sometimes for them as well – and it takes time to repair; sometimes, it's broken forever. The best course of action is to take care of yourself, heal and then release them by sending love and prayers that they will eventually find their way. Try it. You will notice the energy lifts from your body, and you feel lighter! I try to remind myself to *let go and let God*. Leave it up to Him. It is no longer my burden to bear. THEN JESUS CAME IN …

I understand you were very angry yesterday. I am glad you have started to let those feelings drift away. There are a lot of lessons to be learned. Each person is stuck in their own game of being right, and they can't see through the shroud of anger they are cloaked in. People often don't want to share what they are thinking or feeling because they don't know how to articulate as well as you do. That, My dear, is why you have to let it go. Keep your vibration elevated so I can connect and help you.

Don't allow yourself to sink into the depths of despair. Keep notes up if need be to remind you.

He continues . . .

Sometimes things have to be taken away for one to learn. Remember the stock market crash? Humans were getting out of control, gambling with their hard-earned money. They didn't appreciate it, so everyone had to wake up. When one doesn't listen and take action, the outcome is to hit bottom. It is adverse, but if you haven't learned it yet, unfortunately, that's where you need to be. I know your people call it tough love, but it's for your ascension, for without it, you stay stuck and never grow, so what was the point of your being born again? It was a waste of time. You must look into your heart. Whatever happened to that which you know as the Golden Rule? "Do unto others as you would have them do unto you." While man wrote the Bible, and it's their perception, there are tenets and psalms that you will see are the word of God if you read and analyze them. Oh, dear child, do not despair. Remember, I am always with you.

I also know you were worried about your medical tests, but didn't they turn out fine? Why is it that something bad had to happen for you to start taking your medication? Your daughter was right. The doctors don't fill out those prescription pads for their health! So, the blood test results scared you a little, didn't they? Good. It made you take action. Do you see how simple it is? Just keep going, dear one. It will get easier, but remember, I am waiting. Like the psychic medium Christopher told you, I have been waiting a long time for you. By the way, when are you going to pick up your studies? You need to start Reiki, remember? How can I help others if you don't do these things? You need to listen and not put things off. Don't wait for someone to need Me, do it now!

"How come I can feel and hear You, but I can't see You?"

Because for some reason, when you see Me standing there, you watch, and you don't open your mouth, He said, laughing.

"I will next time, I promise!"

Okay. We will try it sometime, but not right now. There are more important tasks at hand. I want to touch on forgiveness again. Debra, all I can tell you is to be patient. Be patient with everyone who crosses your path. Your lesson is to be. It is not your journey, it is theirs, and when the time is right, they will each learn something.

"I don't understand why it is so difficult for people to comprehend this."

Love is truly the only answer. He smiles as He says it, shaking his head. *Some are so stubborn…*

When stress creeps in, please learn how to breathe to teach it to others to calm their inner being. People need to understand this. It is pretty simple. We all can step back and connect. I am always here. Remember that.

You will be able to help others. Do not worry or concern yourself with the path. I will show you every step of the way when it is time. Pay attention for doors to open, thoughts to enter your mind, classes to appear. Those are things for you to be aware of and consider. I am going to use you, dear one. But first, you must finish the book.

"I just want peace."

I understand. Trust me. Trust the process.

"Yes, of course. That is what You always tell me. Okay, I will trust the process."

People trust you, so you need to trust Me. I will guide you. Haven't you experienced that already? Sometimes I know you are amazed at the words that cross your lips. He says, laughing. *Those are My words, my dear, but I would think by now you have learned that.*

The pandemic that hit the planet made everyone slow down. Some people got it; others didn't. I know it helped you more to be able to go within and connect with Me. Some people get so caught up in life and living what they think is real, but none of it matters when it's time to go home. That is what I don't understand. Stuff is just stuff, things you don't really need, yet people continue to spend, and then they get stressed out because they have overspent and have bills to pay, so they have to work longer. They can't retire and enjoy life. They can't make time to connect with Me. I find it quite sad, really. Thankfully you got off that merry-go-round. It took Me one heck of a time, though! You just didn't get it. Money doesn't buy happiness, and it certainly won't buy good health. You realize that now.

"It's interesting," I said, "because my circle of friends or relationships is shrinking, and I am pretty comfortable with that. In the past, having a lot of friends was so important to me, but it's no longer my focus. The quality of the relationships means so much more. My time with You is precious."

Share My word. Give others hope. Tell them that if I can come to you, I can come to them. They just have to be open and believe. Faith came easy for you.

"Well," I said laughing, "of course it did! You were standing at the end of my bunk! What else was I supposed to think!?"

I know, He said, smiling. *It was the perfect storm. Your teenage hormones were raging, and you thought you were in love. You have learned a lot since then.*

"But I still have more to learn about love," I said.

Yes, you do.

"I mean, I can say I love someone, and I believe it with every fiber of my being. However, what I feel for You, and knowing what's waiting for all of us on the other side, is this all-encompassing overwhelming feeling. I cannot put words to it, so it must be an elevated level of love, a love without conditions."

I start thinking . . .

"Ahh, I can love someone if they behave a certain way and aren't self-centered or mean."

Now you are getting it. You love them conditionally. Loving someone without conditions isn't easy, is it?

"Wow. No, it isn't. It's impossible. I think You are the only one capable of unconditional love. I don't believe human beings are capable of that, are we?"

That's tough to say. It could happen, but you have to be a highly enlightened soul. It's okay. Remember, you're not perfect. Life is a school and a game. You learn, and you play. The reward is how you lived the game. Only you will be the judge of that when you come home. Nobody else. He paused. *I realize you are tired. It has been a long week. How about if you rest up and we connect again tomorrow. Sleep well, dear one.*

Surprised that He was aware of that, I said, "Thank you, and good night. I just want to be sure there isn't anything else You need to share. Is there anything?"

No, I can feel your exhaustion. Rest is what you need now.

"Okay. Thank you. This is just so amazing that I can connect with You this way. I still don't know who will believe me, but I can't concern myself with that, can I?"

No, you can't, He said, then He was gone.

DAY TWO

Friday, May 7, 2021

After reciting the Author's Prayer three times, Tom started the morning with the prompt, "I am an author because . . ."

I start typing. "I am an author because I have a gift to share."

"I am an author because *He* wants me to share what *He* is telling me."

"I am an author because Jesus wants you to know these things. So it is not just gibberish that is coming through."

He wants you to know that He is always here for you. All you have to do is trust, go within and believe. Life doesn't have to be a struggle. It is easy, really, and He has a sense of humor. But, remember He is just like us. He was human, just like us, so don't be afraid. He is always here.

He wants you to know that life isn't meant to be a struggle. He wants you to find peace. If you look around, it is everywhere. Yes, He understands we must work to keep food on the table and a roof over our head, but He wants you to connect with Him at the end of the day. You will find peace and harmony with Him if you do. Don't turn to food or alcohol to soothe your stressed mind; use Him to help you.

We are all beings having a human experience. What makes us human? It is our conditioning. Our skin, bones, and organs, but don't you think other beings have similar qualities? Those on earth have the ability for a spiritual understanding if you are open to it. Look around you.

And then I feel Him. He's there, listening to my thoughts.

Many are seeking, He said. *There are many paths to enlightenment; however, there is only one God. One omnipotence. It makes no difference how you get there. Understanding and enlightenment will be yours when it is your time. Just trust the process. Do good. Be kind to others. Be loving. Give up the fight, for there doesn't need to be one. Remember that we are all connected. We are all children of God. If everyone would remember that,* He laughs and shrugs his shoulders, *wouldn't this be a wonderful world!*

"Yes, of course!" I said.

I am sorry for the pain and suffering. I know how it feels. Yet, I want you to understand that pain or suffering opens you up to the oneness we share. You, my dear, know about pain and suffering; however, most of your suffering is in your mind. I have tried for years to get you to understand the purpose of meditation, yet you resisted. I feel as if I have been beating you over the head with messages, but I am thankful that you are now finally getting it.

Why is it that when you receive a thought you don't pay attention? You don't wonder, What was that all about? Start thinking!! Those are messages! Your kind likes to call it intuition, so be it then. But whatever name you choose to use, LISTEN and ACT! Your angels and guides have wanted to shake you over the years, and at times they have given up; they let you go on your path knowing you would reconnect with them someday.

I can hear your thoughts. Don't think that you have wasted time. You needed those experiences to get to this point in your life now. What if you were still asleep? We wouldn't be talking now!

Dear one, you must tune in more. Why you don't go in your Spirit Room is something I don't understand. Please. God is there. I will come, and so will others. You have the door cracked, but now it is time to open it wide so everyone can go in. Trust Me. It will happen. When you are in that room, it will shut out all the outside noise. It is so peaceful and serene. Electronics in your office make it difficult to connect, as the frequency is high and the room vibrates at a different level than we do spiritually. To reach others at the same vibration, you need to have energy flow, and your office is just not the place. There is too much equipment in there.

"Wow! That makes perfect sense. I never thought of that before."

Of course, you didn't, He said, laughing, *That's why I am telling you now.*

I can't believe I am having a conversation with Jesus Christ, and He is talking to me about computers and technology blocking the flow. Who on earth would have thought that!?

"Okay, I will start using my room. It will be a lovely place for me to finish my studies. Now I am excited to go in there. Why, oh why did I wait? Thank you. Thank you. I feel a warmth coming over me as goosebumps rise in my body. And so, it is!"

Dear one, please finish your studies. Get your degree! Why have you put it off? Procrastination isn't a sign of being lazy for you. I feel it's a sign of fear. My dear girl, do not be fearful of anything. I am with you. Sometimes I want to yell because I get frustrated watching you. When you had that reading two weeks ago, did he not tell you that I have been waiting?

"Yes, of course that is what Christopher told me."

Take heed in that. Waste no more time. I have so many things I want to share with you so you can help others. Please allow Me to work through you. Commit to getting these tasks finished and complete. Do you not realize how special our relationship is, or are you just taking Me for granted because I have been with you most of your life?

"No! I am so sorry!" I started crying while looking at His picture. "I'm sorry. I guess part of it is fear, but not what you are thinking. It is the fear of the unknown and how this will all look. I love my family, and I love the space where I am right now, even having this dis-ease. I guess I am fearful as to how I will find balance and be myself. How can I be the old me and still be doing Your work?"

My dear Debra, have I not told you before to trust the process? Will you please write that down and put it on notes, you know, those sticky notes you used years ago. You had them everywhere reminding you to STAY IN THE PRESENT. How, my dear, is this any different?

Nodding, I said, "Okay. Okay!! You are exactly right. I need to shut out the noise and do this! Now I understand why people who truly and completely commit close off the outside world for the time being. It's easier that way. Sometimes it's the only way, so we don't get distracted." I frowned. "Here I go again. Who is going to believe me?"

My dear, how many times are you going to play that on repeat? It does not matter who. It does not matter where. It does not matter why. Remember, some will, and that is all that is important. One at a time, one by one, He said, laughing.

"What's so funny?" I asked.

Well, one by one. What does that remind you of?

"Noah's Ark," I said, laughing.

Yes. Everything in life is one by one. One day at a time. One step at a time. One thought at a time. Think about those struggling with substance abuse. One day at a time. One day at a time, then compounds with the next day, and then it is two, and then one more day, and before you know it has been one month. In fact, you know someone casually who is four months in. He will be a role model for others. You have supported him from a distance. You have watched him. He is a good man. He will help others. He didn't believe in himself, and he struggled with choices he made in the past. He needed to hit bottom. Why do you think he lost that job? If he continued to move up, he would not have learned. He needed that to awaken, and when he did, I was there. The only difference is, he listened. Sadly others don't, and they repeat the cycle until their death.

"Yes. That all makes sense to me now."

Everything is one by one, my dear.

Make a list. One by one, you get things checked off.

One day at a time.

One thought at a time opens you to the thought that will come next.

When you are open, I can come through. When you are open, your family and friends in heaven can come through. When you finish this book, Kate is waiting to help you with the other one. Joy will help you with the third. But you must take these baby steps, one by one, to get there. Do not rush it. Do not think you have failed. Do not think you are wasting time. Everything is in divine timing, and now that you are ready, it will start happening more. Watch, listen, and learn. The lessons will unfold before your very eyes now that I know you have finally gotten it. You have opened up to the Universe. When you take a lunch break today, go into your Spirit Room, turn on the soft lighting you added, listen to the writing music that Tom has given you, and see what comes. Also, please get rid of some of the things in there. Vibrations need to be precise. Clutter blocks them, and they will bounce and reverberate in another direction. Remove items that are on the floor. In the following months, your time will come to empty and deplete the things that will no longer serve you. You will see.

He laughed. *Once again, trust the process. Please put that on a sticky note: "Trust the process!"*

"Okay. I wrote it down in my notebook. I'm not allowed to read any of this until the sessions are over. I am always amazed at what I have written. It is hard to believe they are; no, excuse me, they aren't my words. They are Yours. You know what I mean!"

Yes, I do, He said, smiling.

"It just amazes me that this can happen at all! All those years You have been with me. I'm sorry. I don't mean to get emotional, but…" I shook my head. "…I've wasted so much time."

My dear, you are here now, and that is all that matters.

"Jesus, do You remember when I had those dreams, and they would come true the next day? I am ready and willing if You want me to have them again. I am not afraid. I know You are with me."

Well, weren't you surprised when I told you about the money that was given to your brother?

I remember waking up one morning hearing a voice stating that my mother had written my brother a check for a specific amount of money. *What?? What is that all about and where did that come from?* So, I shared it with my husband and he said to call my mom and ask.

I thought about it over my morning coffee before picking up the phone. This wasn't an easy conversation knowing how she always wants things to be *even* between us. I merely wanted validation. As I talked to my mom, I stumbled through my words, stating I didn't want anything but I just needed to know. Afterall, she was used to my receiving messages. When she replied, "Yes" not only was I stunned that I'd received a message like that, but before I could ask *why*, she told me. Then we argued when she said she was going to send me a check, that I honestly didn't want, until she said, "So what if you get it now or after I am dead? I would like to see your life be easier and it makes me feel good to help you kids."

That message had completely slipped my mind as that was months ago and now Jesus was asking me about it?

"That was You?"

Yes, He said, laughing. *I was testing you to see if you were curious enough to receive validation. I will give you more examples, more tests, so listen and be aware; however, you must meditate daily, My dear. It is the only way to clear your mind of, what do you call it, 'social media?' It fills your mind just as the television and news. I have noticed you no longer read the newspaper. I am impressed, especially since working for a newspaper was your life.*

"But I can't trust or believe what I see written anymore."

Yes, they call it news; however, for you, it is merely a distraction. You do not need to concern yourself with that. There will be a time and a place. Think of Me as your news. Look to Me for clarity and your communication to the inside world. This is now your mission. You fought to help others earn a decent living. You helped hundreds of people. Now you are on a new path. This will be your new mission. I realize your family and friends may have difficulty with it, but those who love and trust you will come around.

He smiled. *Did you notice how quickly your prayer was answered that you asked for your husband?*

"Yes. Thank you, only it was truly unbelievable." I said, laughing. "Whoever would have thought Bill would listen to someone he once shunned? He can be very biased, but my dad was, too. We are all just people. We are all the same. We have a heart and a soul. Just because the package arrives differently doesn't mean we should judge it. When you are open to the possibility you may find that person might have something of value to add. I am glad Bill had that experience. It showed me he's not as old-school as he thinks. Just because something was the way it was doesn't mean it always has to be."

He is a good man. He is willing. I just needed to chip away his hard exterior to get to the softness inside. It's there, you know.

"Yes, of course, I do. I knew it even before I met him! I felt it over the phone."

Sadly, he has been conditioned by outside distractions. Those who report news create it. They think it is news, but it perpetuates the violence.

"When they report the news, why can't they speak up and say that we need a little more love in the world. It's all information that is upsetting."

They think it's their job. Their employer would disapprove. It's just the facts.

"Well, isn't it also a fact to do unto others as you would do unto yourself?"

Yes, He replied forlornly. *But people have forgotten. It is up to us to remind them. It is up to us to awaken them again, and hopefully, this time, they will stay awake.*

"Maybe I should start posting things of that nature."

That would be a good start to create awareness and prepare people for this book.

"Hmmm…you are right. That way, the book won't be coming out of left field. Instead, I will be planting seeds."

He laughed and asked, *Isn't that what you have on your Vision Board?*

"Yes," I said, smiling. "You are exactly right. I will do that today. Thank you. What else do You want me to know?"

Debra dear, tell people not to be afraid. Two months ago, one of your friends came home, yet one is left behind. She is scared. You need to have an open conversation with her.

"I know I do. I will call her. I will find out what she fears. Please help me to find the words to bring her peace."

Meditate before the phone call, and I will be there.

"Thank you. You know, I used to be afraid of dying."

He smiled again. *I know. You were so young. The prayer they had children recite was terrifying. Who would ever want to go to sleep after praying that way!*

"I know! 'If I should die before I wake, I pray the Lord my soul to take.' As a kid, I would be sick to my stomach with fear. I was afraid I wouldn't wake up!"

I am glad they changed it. Prayer should never be fearful.

"I want to ask You something else," I said. "How do You explain science and religion? Which is correct?"

That is quite simple, My dear. God created the earth. Who do you think created dinosaurs? He chuckled. *Humankind came afterward. I realize it has confused many, and they are non-believers, or some don't know what to believe.*

Your daughter struggles with this. She used to believe until school put other notions in her head. She will come around. She's smart. In her heart, she knows I am here. He laughed again. *I mean, who wouldn't? I am real. I lived on the planet. Your daughter has unrealized gifts. She brushes them off, but you and I know differently. She took the easy road with her career. She has a gift. She can help and heal others just as you do, only she intuitively knows. Intuitively you would see. We all have different senses. Some are defined more than others. I am glad to see you are working on opening all of yours. Look at what you can do now! Seeing used to be your only gift! Now you know, feel, and hear.*

I would like to have the sense of *smell*. I want to smell my father's cologne. I want to smell my grandmother's pineapple upside-down cake.

In time, My dear. In time. Trust the process.

"Yes, I know! I am sick of trusting the process!" I said, laughing. "I want it all now!"

Don't you think I realize that? Good things are worth waiting for.

"Now, don't You go giving me that old cliché! You are Jesus."

Indeed, I am, but there is a process. One by one, remember?

"Okay. Yeah. I forgot. One by one."

Be grateful, dear one.

"But I am!"

No, You're not. Practice gratitude. Look at us! We are now talking! It took over fifty years for us to converse so You could hear me.

"Yes. I was always just petrified and in awe at the sight of You! I was mesmerized. I never knew I could speak to You. I know that is entirely ridiculous, but who would think You can carry on a conversation with Jesus! Besides, I was probably afraid if I spoke, You might disappear."

Yes, maybe, but you never tried.

"Wow." I laughed. "Okay. You are right. Thank You for coming to me that morning and speaking. That was the best gift You could have given me. I didn't see You, but I felt You and knew You were there. I heard You. I believe that is the day I realized that two-way communication was possible. I mean, I thought I'd be writing this book about the story of my encounters with You! Never in a million years did I think that You would be helping me write the book! I still find it unbelievable. Well, no, I do believe it because it is happening to me. I feel You as I look at Your picture, yet Your words are coming through my fingers.

Who do you think wrote "I am a Healer" on that piece of paper in Sedona at Bell Rock?

"I wrote it."

Yes, you wrote it automatically, but where did you think the thought came from?

"Well, at the time, I didn't know. It shocked me, actually. I mean, I never thought of myself as a healer."

I know, so you justified it with your words.

"Yes, my words can help heal and bring comfort."

And so can I. You'll see. Do the work. Christopher was the messenger. I know you were upset that you had to wait two months to see him, but it divinely unfolded as it should, don't you now agree?

"Yes! Gee, do You always have to be right?"

Laughing, He replied, *Yes.*

You are good at listening. You understand. You trust your intuition. I will guide you. Have no fear, He said.

I told Him, "There have been times I have been so frustrated that I just wanted to go home. Sometimes life seems so hard."

I know. I realize that, however, it is not your time. You allow this drama to create problems for you. It would be best to create a ritual to wash it away and release it when it appears. Don't let it in. Everyone is here for whatever lessons are necessary. They need to go through them individually. You cannot fix them so let it be. Sure, it may be sad or painful, but just like it is your journey, it is also theirs. I want you to find peace in the process. Anger doesn't do anyone any good. It keeps you stuck from evolving, but then you are already aware of that. Life is good, Debra dear. Life is good, yet it can also be awful. It is what you make it. You have finally reached the pinnacle. You have realized that money is to assist you in living. You don't need all these things. I will provide. Please don't waste it. Do unto others. Give unto others. Be a gift and a blessing to others. That is how you will serve. Just connect with Me, and I will lead you. Trust the process.

I would never have thought I could connect with Him in this manner, nor would I have thought He had a personality like this and a sense of humor! He is funny. It brings me comfort that not only will my family and loved ones be waiting for me when it is my time to cross through the veil, but I know now that Jesus will be standing there, and it gives me joy beyond comprehension! Thank you, God. Thank you, Jesus. I love You and am so grateful for this journey with You.

DAY THREE

Saturday, May 8, 2021

After our usual start to the session, reciting the Author's Prayer three times, Tom has us take a couple deep breaths and then says, "Fifty things. Count them down. This should be easy.

Write things you are grateful for. Your heart, lungs, blood, oxygen, animals, parents, trees..."

"No thinking allowed. Only feeling." Tom reminds us. "Keep it going. I am thankful for the following…This should be easy. Then when you are done with that, go back into your writing and GO! Nice… Remember to smile… Keep typing… Smile dammit!" as he watches us on Zoom and laughs. "It's okay to laugh. Type like the wind. The wind beneath my wings… Feel it."

My fingers effortlessly fly across the keyboard. I am thankful for Jesus. I am grateful knowing that I can connect with Him anytime. Why, oh, why didn't I realize that before? Why did I think it had to be in this class? Oh, for God's sake! I can talk to Him anytime, but writing is so much easier. I can easily connect with Him in this way. There is no reason to struggle with anything. Why haven't I seen that before? I'm sorry. I'm so sorry.

Dear one, I understand. You aren't of the clergy or a nun. I would expect that you would have a more challenging time, but I have been here. Think back. I have been here!

"Yes, You have. It is insanely crazy that when I struggled, I didn't connect with You. Wait! Is that what You want me to do? Do You want me to show people that they have this ability as well?"

He is laughing. *Well, that would be a good idea now, wouldn't it?*

"Oh my God! Oops. I am sorry! Why is that just a phrase everyone uses? It's even an acronym now: OMG."

I know.

"Okay, okay. I get it. I already know I don't need to ask *how*. I know You will show me the way. You will put teachers in my path to show me how to do this. Wait. Wait. I will need to meditate on this one. It is so strange that I pick up signals and messages so much easier when I open up and clear my head."

What do you think I have been trying to tell you?

"By the way, thanks for the great nights' sleep. I am still struggling with my tooth."

Don't worry. It will settle down. Have faith. He paused. *What are you feeling?*

"I feel tenseness." I thought about it for a moment. "Yes, fear. My chest feels heavy like there is a weight on it, which is hard to imagine because I am sitting, and if there were a weight, it would drop into my lap!"

Tell me about the fear.

Again, I just sat there, contemplating what to say next. Then, as I take a deep breath, I said, "I'm afraid to put myself out there, You know?"

Why? Think of it as serving the people. Think of it as union organizing. Think of it as your passion. When something is your passion is it not something you go after?

"Yes. I guess I am feeling this way because I can't see the outcome."

I understand. You always want to see things. What about when you designed the greeting cards? Was that not just an idea, and you ran with it?

"Yes, but it failed."

After I had breast cancer I received a *message* to design and create cancer greeting cards. I had a vision, just not the steps to get there. It was a fabulous idea because nobody had them! It ended up being a great learning experience but unfortunately, I didn't listen, or at the time was not aware of the messages to guide me! Now that He brought it up, I start reflecting...

My dear one, stop. You are not focusing. I hear your thoughts. You are rambling again.

"But those are my thoughts, and that is why I have the fear."

I am not suggesting you jump in. I am suggesting you talk to one of your mentors and see what is possible. But, of course, just because you speak to them, it doesn't mean you have to do it, right?

"You are too funny, and how is it that You make sense all the time?"

Really? He asked, laughing. *"You're asking Me that?"*

"Oh. No. I guess not. I mean, You *are* Jesus." I laughed. "You know, I didn't think we would be connecting again this morning."

Why not? Isn't that why you are here?

"Well, yes, but I wanted to revise the book."

There is plenty of time for that. You need to spend time with Me today. You can revise the book when you are not in class. When your home is quiet and peaceful, it is the best time to connect with Me. So let's take advantage of that, at least until you get into your Spirit Room. It is lovely, by the way. The energy in the room is incredible. Thank you for creating it. I am honored.

"When am I supposed to work on the other book?"

That time will come, My dear.

"When I am revising this book, I need to shift back and forth between books. So maybe we can experience that process together? I know You said yesterday that Kate would help me with that book. I know why. Kate should have written her own book, and if she had lived longer, I would have continued to encourage her. Who knows? I may write it for her. I always thought a title 'Ask Kate,' modeled after Dear Abby might have been good."

Kate had come into my life when my biological clock was ticking and I knew if I didn't figure things out, I would never be destined for motherhood. "Debbie" really had baggage. Sadly, she was terrified of abandonment and, oh, this is embarrassing, she felt she had to have a man in her life to be complete. (The old Cinderella story.) Debbie's *picker* was off and she kept attracting the wrong men to her. (Notice how I speak of her in the third person.) Kate helped me leave "Debbie" behind and become Debra, who is empowered, confident, and a strong woman. I banked on every word Kate said, and moved with lightning speed to change. Within one year I had become a version of who I am today. Debbie is someone I would like to forget, but because of her I know there are many others like her who I can help. That was the book I had set out to finish!

"That is of course until You interrupted me!" I told Him. "I now know that You will help me, too, won't You?"

Of course, I will. Remember, dear Debra, I am always here.

"I'm sorry. I know I sound like a broken record. It's still hard to imagine that You are talking to me. It was one thing to have my dad come through, but *You?*"

He looks at me and smiles. *We have work to do, My dear.*

"I am grateful that I can connect with You. I am grateful for the opportunity to teach others how to connect with You."

You are the messenger, My dear. You are to show people the way. Lead them to Me. Just lead them to Me, and I will do the rest. All it takes is one person to connect with Me. First, they will tell someone about your book and their experience, someone they trust and who trusts them, and then that person will follow. It just takes one. Remember, one by one.

"Right," I laughed, "like Noah's ark."

Yes, exactly. Trust the process. Trust the process, my dear.

"Did you see I made post-it notes today with TRUST THE PROCESS written on them?"

Of course, I did. You took the first step. Just as people will come, one by one, you will take one step after the other to reach your goal. Just remember, I am here to support you. Anytime you need Me or want to talk, just sit down and start writing about gratitude over and over. I will hear it. I will come. Okay?

"Okay. Thank you. Wow. I feel Your love vibrating through every cell in my body."

Good. That is how I want you to feel.

That weekend was one of the most beautiful and overwhelming times in my life. When it was over, it took some time for me to reflect and take it all in. I knew when I sat down and read what I had written, I would once again be mesmerized by all that was said, and though I still may not completely understand, I would most definitely trust the process!

CHAPTER NINETEEN

MORE MESSAGES & HEAVEN

Thursday August 19, 2021

Two months later, I was still processing the experience I had at the writing retreat in May. The temperatures were starting to heat up in Arizona, and while most of the country was just beginning to thaw from winter, Phoenicians were taking this time to enjoy their pools, hike, or do other outdoor activities. The weather was perfect, but now in August, the triple-digit days of summer have descended upon us!

As I went about my normal routine, the next writing retreat was never far from my thoughts. I would often catch myself thinking, *Can He really come through and talk to me again? It just seems so impossible.* Each time I would hear Him say, with laughter in His voice, *Trust the Process* and I too would chuckle.

The first day of the retreat I was filled with nervous anticipation when Tom gave us the prompt. We were to repeatedly ask ourselves, "Where am I going with this book? I want you to see God in your mind."

My fingers started to fly, and I was again stunned by what appeared on the screen: "On a journey with God. Jesus is here guiding me. I cannot fail. I am divinely led."

"Go with the flow. You're doing great." Tom said encouragingly.

"I have been waiting for you, I joked silently, "It's about time you showed up. "

I came to you a couple of weeks ago. Now is the time. I will have you share your story and help erase people's fears about where we are eventually going. There is no reason to be afraid. I am with them. I am the Son of God. I am always with you. There truly is life everlasting, and I will show you. Have no fear. I realize that some may not believe you and think you are a little off, but after they read this book, I hope the dim light will start to flicker until it is shining brightly so when it is their time, they will see that light and remember what I told them through you.

When it is time for you to leave the earthly plane, you will see helpers. They may be family members across the veil or your guardian angels. You may even motion to them, and your family will wonder what you are doing as you wave or reach out. Your soul will lift out of your body, and you will see a white light once you have left your room. The white light will illuminate the way. Some will see a tunnel, while others see a long staircase or a path. It's whatever vision you expect to see so that you are comfortable. You will intuitively know that it is okay to follow. Start by taking that first step in your mind. Do not be afraid.

"But what if they see their family grieving and crying?" I asked.

Yes, it is only natural to look back and say goodbye to your body lying there. You will see family members upset. Everyone experiences this, but it is time for you to come home. Trust Me. We are going on a journey. I am here, as are all the family and friends who crossed over before you. They are waiting to greet you. It is like a celebration. You are coming home. However, some will feel remorse and stay with their family for a while. If you see someone calling a family member to tell them you have passed, you can quickly transport yourself to their home so you can say goodbye. You cannot concern yourself with their tears.

Remember when Keith came home? He woke you at six thirty-five a.m., five minutes or so after he had passed, to tell you to reach out to his wife, Mary Kay. Remember how shocked you were?

"Yes, I thought it was just a dream. That is until I went to work, and I heard people talking, asking others if they remembered the guy with the gray ponytail who always gave out bubble gum. I was shocked and started crying when they said that he passed this morning! I couldn't believe that! Then I remembered my *dream!*"

I had met Keith when I started working at America West. He was sixteen years older than me, yet we had an instant connection spiritually. His wife Mary Kay was the love of his life and fifteen years his junior. Keith was Native American and an incredible artist. A very humble man, he never spoke much about his paintings when we worked at the airline, however, I would visit him when the town of Fountain Hills held their art shows so I could catch up with my old friend without the constraints of work and see what he had been up to. I never knew, until after his passing, how famous Keith Winterhawk Adams was as an artist, and I knew none of our coworkers did either.

Keith passed on September 3, 2010, and I was still a newbie on my spiritual path, yet I reflected on this incredible dream I had awoken to that morning and needed to know more. I immediately went to his home after work. I had no idea that he'd been so sick.

"I felt bad that I wasn't there for him," I said.

My dear, He didn't want you to be. He wanted you to remember him as he was. But, he came to you. He chose to tell you in the way that he did, and you listened.

"Yes, I even spoke to him. I mean, I was asleep, so I'm sure my lips weren't moving, but I kept saying, 'Okay, Keith. I'll call Mary Kay. I'll check on Mary Kay,' but then I fell back asleep."

Only five minutes had passed before he visited you, and it may not seem as if he was with his family very long, but there is no thought of "time" as we know it. He also knows he can be with his wife anytime he chooses. All you have to do is think of them, and you're there. They need to learn this process that all humans must go through. Remember when you lost a loved one how it felt? It hurts, yes, but you finally made your peace with it and kept the love for them deep inside your heart.

"Yes, but the grieving process can be long for some."

Little by little, with the evolution of spiritual knowledge, it will be easier on those suffering. But, unfortunately, it takes losing someone you deeply love to make one start searching for answers.

Dear one, you have a gift, and it is time for you to tap into it. You can bring comfort to those who are grieving by your connection with the other side. I want to take you on a journey, so you see where you are going to help bring peace to those living on the planet. You need to trust your intuition and the guidance I give you. Do not worry. Do not allow fear to enter into any of this. I will show you the way. I know that ability is yours if you choose. You only need to trust and be open. Spirits are just not going to appear and startle you. It does not work that way. Remember, just last month I finally spoke to you. You always sat and stared at Me. You never spoke. We will get to a place where you can not only see Me but speak to Me. I want you to ask Me questions, so think of them and don't worry. Follow Me now. Follow Me, and I will give you a glimpse of what is waiting.

Preparing for the meditation, my fingers poised on the keyboard, I sat back, closed my eyes and took a few long deep breaths, getting relaxed in preparation for the guided journey to unfold. With each deep breath in and exhale, I sank deeper into my chair. My shoulders started to soften and a wave of serenity flowed through my body. Expecting to see a tunnel, I noticed a staircase in the distance. Once we climbed the stairs, we stepped out into a glorious meadow. I was surprised that I didn't experience difficulty breathing, which is a side effect of my monthly injection. In retrospect, maybe it's because I was following Him in my mind and not actually doing it!

Looking around, I noticed that the colors were as I remembered when my dad visited. They were so vibrant, like nothing you have ever seen. Birds were snuggled together on the treetops and singing such a sweet melody. The sun was shining, and it felt so peaceful. As we continued walking, He opened a door so that we could enter a room. The building was white with glass walls so I could look and see the surroundings. I was shaking my head in amazement, for it was truly the biggest adventure one could ever experience.

Remember how you felt driving the race car? He asked. *Well, this will be the same adrenaline as you look around and see all that is before you, but it is in a different peaceful form of contentment. You, My dear, have arrived. This is the "other side." This is what you call Heaven. This is the paradise waiting for everyone. Look around. You can see the fields on one side, and then as you turn to your right, you will see buildings. That is where classrooms are. It is a place for you to learn. Here you graduate and go on to the next level.*

I looked on in amazement.

"But where are the people?" I asked. "I was hoping to see some of my family."

Patience, dear. Not now. This is our time.

He paused. *I must tell you; I find it interesting that humans think angels actually have wings and fly around. They are spirits, clothed in robes of different colors and hues or clothing you may be familiar with, and are here to teach. Some people choose to stay here while others decide later; they want to go back.*

"Why do people want to go back?" I asked.

I liken it to a mortal mind. You go through early education and then extended learning in what you call college, where there are different degrees you can attain. Then, with the vast knowledge, you can help empower others.

Dear one, you know you are supposed to spend your life being of service to others. You have known that for a long time, and you have done a great job, but now it is time for you to take it further. It is time for you to share your friendship with Me. So many people followed you and trusted you. You have integrity, and they know you are honest. Do you wonder why people can open up to you so freely? Just look at your heart and compassion. People are not afraid to share their innermost feelings with you. They know you will keep their trust. You have had many professions where you had to honor that trust. You had responsibilities in past careers to gain that trust, and now it is time to step into this one.

"But I am the most unlikely person to be able to do this," I said.

Oh, My dear, no, you are not. Have I not been coming to you since you were just a teen? I heard your pleas and made sure you saw Me because how would you believe I existed without seeing Me? I understand that faith is hard. I know the churches and temples teach about faith, and we are supposed to believe the one on the pulpit, but sometimes those we trusted do not have God in their hearts. They have hurt others. They have done things indescribable to our youth, so why would they then actually believe I am real?

"It is because they know You are real," I replied. "There are pictures of You everywhere. You are on the cross at their church."

But you must realize that they are not like you. I cannot just appear. Most people would think their minds were playing tricks on them. So many people are hurting. The world is in such disarray right now. I need to have My voice heard to bring peace and comfort. I know you do not understand, and you wonder, "Why me?" But why not you? I already know you and have had a long relationship with you. I have gotten you through both cancers, and I am sorry you had to go through breast cancer to have validation from someone else that I was real. I know it was a great relief after all these years, but once your therapist saw Me, that completely erased any doubt in your mind, and after that, I returned more often. My dear, I can come anytime. All you have to do is ask for Me or even think of Me. I know that having your therapist see Me also makes it more credible and believable when you share My story. Just look at yesterday when your girlfriend teared up when you shared this. People need to hear Me. I do not want them to have any fear. I realize you are waiting for your path, but first, we need to connect more deeply so I can help you to help them. I don't want people to suffer. Some medications can help, but it's the cycle of life.

"Then why do some suffer? It is awful!" I exclaimed.

Dear one, there is a reason for everything, just as they chose the family to experience the life lessons and experiences they were supposed to. Yes, it is painful, but usually, medication can alleviate some of it. Yes, it is hard to watch someone in pain, but people need to learn compassion and empathy. Sometimes we need to experience what pain is to learn about all the human emotions and feelings. I know it hurts. How do you think I felt when they nailed Me to the cross? I know there is heartache, but we do survive. We move on. There are lessons for every single person whose life is touched by this. I realize it is hard to understand. But, that is where trust and faith come in. You have seen heaven. You know where you are going; that is why you are not concerned, nor are you afraid. You've seen your father and brother Steven. You know they are together. Think about your brother. I realize he was an infant, but you could not get a good look at him when you first visited here after your father passed. Could you look at him now? Look at him and see his face.

I don't know why it surprised me when Steven suddenly appeared, but it did. My eyes locked on my brother, noting that he seemed to be in his early thirties, though he would have been twenty years older than that if he had lived.

I know. You thought your brother would be older, but I didn't want him to be too old, Jesus said, laughing. *You wouldn't recognize him then. You had to see the family traits.*

Understanding, I nodded my head.

Your grandparents are over to your right.

As I looked, I saw them in these woven rockers with the aluminum frames they used to have on their deck.

"How can that be?" I asked.

My dear, anything that was familiar to you in your life before can be created here by imagining it as being so. Your father already told you that, remember?

He paused. *I must tell you there is one thing that troubles Me. No, make that two. The first is I do not understand why people say they are God-fearing. Why on earth should they ever fear My father? There is nothing to fear. I don't appreciate it when the leaders of churches plant that seed. Do they think if people fear God, it will make them behave in a good manner? You were all created in My image. Pure, perfect, and with a big heart. As children, you learn to fear. You learn bad traits that will not serve you, possibly by your parents, or hear stories that are not true. Your surroundings, your friends, and your environment can hold many mistruths. They run like a tape on repeat throughout your life unless you change it. God-fearing is ridiculous. Somehow, we need to get the message across that people should never fear God. I also don't like the term Judgment Day. What on earth are these people doing to My flock? Why put fear in them? There is no Judgment Day by God or Me. If you want to call it Judgment Day, then you must realize that you, dear one, are the only person judging yourself. There is no such thing. The new agers call it akashic records, but the reality is it is nothing more than a review of your life on earth. You get to take a look back on your experiences of your time on the planet. There will be many happy times; however, you will also see and feel some of the heartache you went through as well as the heartache you caused. The only reason you are reviewing this is to see what you may have changed, what you learned, and if you so choose to return, what you can do better next time. However, please know the choice is yours. You do not have to return unless deep within your conscious you feel you need to.*

Then, as if He'd had a sudden revelation, Jesus laughed.

I could say deep within your heart; however, the heart is an earthly term, and you shed that when you come here.

There is no one here to judge you, so please tell people to not worry. And while I mention it, what is this notion of Hell that people are so afraid? There is no Hell. You create the hell in your mind and within your energy until you can resolve it for things you have done while on the earthly plane. There is no devil with a pitchfork. Someone created that in an attempt to scare you into being good. He laughed again. *That is ridiculous. You put yourself in hell; however, you can free yourself from that. Only you can release the bondage of that existence. It is once again another way to make you fearful or scare you into behaving in a godly manner.*

In reflection, He laughed again. *Nobody can behave in a godly manner because they aren't GOD. Yes, they can be good and kind and have compassion for others. I found it most disheartening that many were taught the Golden Rule as children but seemed to forget about it. I thought it was so simple. "Treat others as you wish to be treated." That is what saddens Me most in your world. The killing and riots, wars, and hurting people. Why would they do that if they did not want it in return? That is what the Golden Rule is. I see you shaking your head. The Golden Rule. Is it that hard? Is it that difficult? It makes Me sad to see such evil on the planet. I have witnessed countless times where someone has committed a crime, and it is their time to come home. Once they leave their body, see the white light with the staircase ... a white fog-like mist gently swirling on each step as they climb, and when they reach the top, an oasis in view. That is when all the hatred is left behind. I have virtually seen them break down and cry for their misgivings and the pain they have caused. They did not mean to do it. They just lost their way. That is why we have to learn forgiveness, but I will explain that later. So, when these people come and are in awe of what they see before them, they realize that. It is as if they shut a door on their evil past and walked into a place of complete serenity. When they experience their life review, they not only see how they wasted their time on the planet my father created for them, but they experience and feel the pain they caused. I know you may have read that there are many mansions in heaven. There are different levels. They come in at a lower level where they need to learn from their mistakes. They need to become more God-like and see good. How long they stay on each level is entirely up to them, but I have seen people move quickly through their coursework so they can graduate and move up.*

"How many lifetimes do we have?" I asked

My dear, as many as you want to experience. It is entirely up to you.

"Why do we have to revert to being old and sick and sometimes be in diapers as an elderly adult?"

My dear, is it not how it was when you came in? The human body can only last so long. It starts to deteriorate. Just look at how the earth was one hundred years ago. There were no substances to put in food to extend their life. We ate from the land to get the nourishment we needed. Then people evolved and learned about tobacco and alcohol, and drugs. When I hear people say it's the work of the devil, I laugh. No. It isn't. It is just humanity that has evolved and created these things. It is your choice to put them in your body, but if you do, it makes Me sad because some sink to the depths of despair from them, ultimately die, and bring extreme pain to not only themselves but also their family and friends. They are merely substances on the planet. When humanity does involve them, it is your choice alone. You can choose not to use them. You can choose to honor your body and all its greatness to support you in living the best healthy life possible. The choice is yours.

"I find this all very interesting," I said.

Debra, you are to be a voice to help others with some of the lessons they came here to learn. I understand you have tried, but I do not want you to waste time on those who do not choose to listen to you. If you do not see the light start to glimmer, then do not waste any more time and move on. I will have someone else cross your path. I know that it fills your soul and heart with joy. There will be others.

You were exactly right with this current cancer diagnosis. How else were you going to slow down? Toxic environments are unhealthy. Yes, you were serving others by helping with their livelihood, but it started to consume you. It was as if you shut the world off spiritually. Sometimes one has to be knocked off their feet to truly listen. You have that Spirit Room, and you don't utilize it. Go there and meditate. It is a lovely room. I will come.

Many are closed off and do not believe they can receive messages, but I wanted to use you since you do. Please spread your story and share Me with them. I am here, always. I do not want people to be afraid. I am hoping that, one by one, others will share their stories of My visits. The more people who do that will help bring hope to humans, and their faith will return. Why do you think some have what you call near-death experiences? It is so people can see what heaven is and report back. It's just another dimension. The staircase or the tunnel is a metaphor for the unenlightened souls to get there. However, they need something to follow. Debra, they will see the light and be transported. Continue to share the tunnel or staircase, which will be their first point of reference. It will make them feel more comfortable with an inner knowing that it is safe to go. I need people to have faith.

He laughed and said, *Isn't it interesting how you have seen the word "faith" everywhere? Did you just think it was a coincidence, My dear? No, it was a message. I want you to realize that the messages I send come in different ways. Some you notice while others are more subtle, yet they are still messages.*

"Subtle is an understatement!" I said, shaking my head. "I bought several signs that say *faith* to give as gifts because I was drawn to it and wanted people to have faith. Only then I realized it might be the name of this book!"

"I know how hard it is to have faith when you have not seen it, but once you have *seen* like I have been fortunate enough to experience, faith becomes something you just *know*." I am smiling just thinking about it. "It is a given, and nothing else matters."

"My God," I said, then laughed and apologized to the reference, "but I never in a million years thought this was where the writing would take me today. You have been coming to me for over fifty years, and I never once spoke to You." I shook my head. "I never even realized it until a couple of months ago when You were in my bedroom. Yet I *knew* You were there. In retrospect, I need to know more about the theta state of mind. Maybe that is where I can connect more as I shut the door on the outside world and go within. I cannot believe I never spoke to You! I guess I was in such awe of Your presence that it left me speechless! When I reflect on those experiences, I shake my head. So many missed opportunities to have a conversation with You, but I guess I just wasn't ready."

A deep revelation hit, and I started to cry. "Oh my God, that is why You came now! Thank You. Thank You. You were there for me to ask questions, but I guess I just didn't think it was possible. I realize now how ridiculous that is. All I had to do was ask! Trust me, I heard You loud and clear when You said to give the book away!"

I laughed through my tears then. Trust me? Like I need to say that to Jesus?

He laughed too. *You do realize that some may think, "Debra Ewing? Seriously? She was that union organizer who some called vicious, and who fought for equal rights for workers. Debra, let me touch on that. Many are like lost souls, like the lambs following the shepherd. I know you have never read the Bible. I know you don't understand it, and I also know you just bought a version of it and have yet to open it, so let Me tell you that sometimes the journeys we take are similar to what is in the Bible. You were the shepherd. You spoke the truth. You gave these people hope. Of course, they were going to follow and believe you, just like the lambs. They were your flock. You took care of them, fed them, nurtured them, and now they are fine. Just as you did with that, you will repeat that with this book.*

"Ohhh. It's just so overwhelming to me. I hope people will believe me. I cannot make this stuff up. Shepherd? Really? I have not thought of that phrase since I was a small child in Sunday school."

Debra, My dear, you will be fine. Just trust the process. Please write that down and put it on post-it notes. Isn't that what you tell troubled souls to do that are hurting when you tell them to stay in the present?

"Yes," I replied, laughing.

I want you to write TRUST THE PROCESS and put it in several places in your home. I also want you to schedule those classes for your degree. But, Debra, you know better! It will give you more knowledge and the ability to go deeper spiritually. You will also have more credibility so people who don't know you will be able to trust you just like you did when you met Joy, the ordained minister, many years ago. You felt safe with her, right?

He smiled then, as He knew He was correct.

You need to schedule these classes and do them! Why do you think I put them before you?

It wasn't just something to be a pretty notion or idea. It was to further you along your path. Do the work! My dear, trust Me when I say that your path is already defined. You just have not seen the complete picture yet. That is because I want you to focus on what is in front of you. I want you to trust the process. You need to trust these steps. I want you to actually complete the items and then see what is there before you. Every single thing is a stepping stone, my dear. Take the steps! It will lead you to complete peaceful fulfillment. Trust Me. It is all there.

He continued, *Why do you think you butted heads with a team member at your union hall? You know what I am talking about, yet rather than going with the flow, your ego stepped in and made you push back. Ego is not attractive, My dear. I like that they have made an acronym out of it in My father's name. It is perfectly true. When you are in a place of the ego, you are not in a divine state of being. When you are not in a divine state of being, only negative things can enter. Unfortunately, good comes with the bad, but think about all the hostility and push back when trying to do good. I know you like to finish a campaign you started. I know you like the feeling of accomplishment. You did it with the union. But what keeps you from doing that with other things in your life? Why do you put yourself through so much? Why do you not take care of your body? You only get one in this current lifetime.* He smiled. *You're not one to just sit around. Pick up the books.*

When you look at your vision board, do you see the things you have already set in motion and that you are creating? He asked. *I understand that you do not believe you are capable of doing those things, but My dear, you are. I know that you can help heal wounds when others are suffering. I know you seem confused about which path to take, but you were correct when you said you know I will show you the way. I will, just as I am right now. Do not try to rush the process, dear. Take baby steps. Each step you take builds on another, and before you know it ...* He laughed ... *you'll be looking back. You will see how far you have come. You have this time. Utilize it wisely.*

I can hear your mind saying, "For God's sake." He shook his head. *Yes, of course, if that is what will spur you into action. Get on it right after this retreat. I will be watching, and I am not saying that to make you feel guilty if you fail one day. Set a realistic expectation to follow. Didn't I just give you one yesterday?* He asked, laughing at this thought.

"Oh my God! I am sorry. It is a reference I typically say when the light bulb is blinding me."

He laughed again and said, *Go to class from ten to two Monday through Thursday, like your friend Alena said she was going to do. Just pick a schedule and commit to it. Do you now see how all these little ideas are messages?*

I put my hands to my head. Unbelievable! "You are so right. Some of the messages are so subtle that I don't see them. I need to be more mindful of that!"

There are no accidents, dear one. One step progresses to the other, and before you know it, you will have your degree and be ordained.

"But I don't see myself as a minister," I said. "I have no idea what I will do with it."

Don't worry about the vision. Focus on the paper. Focus on the certificate. Once you are there, that door will open. Trust the process.

I laughed out loud and shook my head. "I truly didn't expect You to have a sense of humor."

Why not? He asked. *I have waited all these years to talk to you, and thankfully it has happened. I knew I couldn't just jump in in this manner. That is why I visited you earlier, telling you to finish the book!* He said, laughing. *What do you think we are doing now?*

Oh my God, I thought as I laughed. "Nobody will believe this."

Yes, they will, He reassured me.

"You're right," I said, laughing. "Of course, they will. There is so much pain and arguing over belief systems, the pandemic, and the political landscape. But, for God's sake, the electronic version of the book is free, so at the very least why wouldn't they want to read a feel-good story even if they don't initially believe it? I have to charge for the paperback versions to recoup some of this cost. I hope You don't mind. I do not want to make anything from this. My goal has always been about faith. Anything extra will be donated. I know You will guide me.

Exactly. Of course, I will. You are planting seeds just like you have in the seed packets on your vision board.

"Oh my God, this is just too much," I exclaimed as the light bulb went off in my head, "I have the picture on my wall! How did you know?" Then I added. "Well, that's a dumb question. You know everything."

Continue planting seeds. Maybe you will plant one hundred, and if twenty-five has a light that flickers, plant some more. Do you see how it can spread? That is why you must give it away. People will be curious, and they have nothing to lose by picking it up. Once they start reading it, curiosity will kick in, so let's see what happens!" He laughed. *Won't that be grand?*

"I apologize. I still can't believe I am having this conversation with You. I watched *Conversations with God*, and I have Neale Donald Walsh's books … yet somehow, I still need to feel like my brain is intact."

I know, He said, *Just as I know you never read the books, yet you bought them.*

"I don't fully understand why I do that," I replied.

It is because the title grabs you and entices you, but you like to see things in pictures, and there are no pictures in adult books. Unfortunately, in your case, your mind wanders. If the author cannot fully capture you, you give up too easily. However, a few authors have piqued your curiosity, and you have finished a couple of their books.

"Yes, Suzanne Giesemann, because who on earth would not believe what she writes! A Commander in the Navy is about as credible as you can get!"

Now, do you understand why you must finish your schooling? It's about credibility, dear one. Educate yourself.

"Why don't you call me by my given name?" I asked.

Because I didn't give it to you. All my flock is dear, He said. *You may have noticed that occasionally I did call you by your birth name, however.*

"Do you talk to others as well?" I asked.

Yes. I visit in different ways. Some listen, see, or know, and others feel My presence yet to carry on a conversation with you; after all these years, I am grateful.

"Will You physically manifest before me again?

Yes, when I feel the time is right. It takes a lot of energy to visit. When you had a troubled youth, I knew I had to shake you up by physically being present; otherwise, who knows what would have happened? I knew you had gifts, so I was patient. I wanted you always to remember My visits.

"Why did you stop?" I asked.

Because it is easier to come to younger people or children. They do not have the fear that adults do. Let Me ask you, would you not be shocked if you saw Me standing at the end of your bed?

Laughing, I said, "Yes."

I remembered when my girlfriend Tonya's husband passed. Mike was such a sweetheart, and we were all devastated. He had gone through a bone marrow transplant five years earlier, and once you pass the five-year mark, you're supposed to be home free. Sadly that was not the case for Mike. They were living on an island off the coast of Alaska, so he had to be medevacked to Seattle. Unfortunately, he didn't make it. I remember Tonya (who I called TJ) telling me that she had to fly home alone. Here you think you will be flying home with your husband, and you don't. I just couldn't imagine!

Mike and TJ had a young son, Evan. She called me one day concerned about him because he was talking to the wall. I don't remember exactly what she shared; however, I knew Mike was visiting him. Initially, she was afraid of what was going on and thought he might need to see a therapist. I believe I suggested she possibly talk with a minister if she felt close enough to one, but not to worry. Evan just had spiritual visits from his daddy on the other side.

Well, now you have your answer, He said, reading my thoughts. *I know it is easier for you to see visually to retain things. I remember when I first came, and you reached out to touch Me. Do you remember that?*

"How could I forget! Why didn't you stay? You left! You could have hung around. I was just a kid."

I just wanted you to know I was there. I felt your guilt, yet I find it interesting that you had a knowing that I was there to make things okay and not throw you further into despair. One would typically feel more guilt in a situation like that, but you, however, just knew. *That was the day I knew you would be open to your gifts. That is why you must go deeper and learn more. You need to trust the process. I know you are afraid of connection with other spirits, but what do you think I am?* He laughed, then added, *You can hear Me. You can see Me. It is just the same, and you can give others such peace.*

"Yes, but what if I fail?"

Tsk, tsk. The only failure is in not trying. You know that! You must trust the process. You need to practice. It is the only way you will know. I have had people talk to you about your gifts. You have seen them firsthand. I want you to focus on the feeling of being able to give the comfort someone needs by connecting with a loved one on the other side. Feel it.

He paused. *How did you feel when your dad or your grandfather came to you? Imagine you describing that for someone else. Now that is joy.*

Thinking about what He said, I asked, "What am I supposed to do with hypnosis or past life regression? I thought that was what I was supposed to learn how to do."

It was something that interested you, and you now know. Just because you learned how to do something doesn't mean you have to make a profession out of it. It also does not mean that you are a failure because you did not follow through with it.

He paused, as if to come up with an example, then laughed. *You drove a race car, right? Experiencing that doesn't mean you need to become a race car driver.*

"Okay. I get it. I am here to learn, and I may learn about numerous things that interest me; however, it doesn't mean that it has to be a lifelong path."

No, it doesn't. Just finish getting your degree. That is the next step.

While you are doing that, I also want you to work on the other book to help women, but you know men suffer from that, too. So many people feel unworthy and end up dissatisfied in relationships out of fear. I find it sad that they do not know how to be themselves and trust the process. I just don't know what to do. That is why I want you to give this book away. You share My message, and hopefully, people may realize that any subsequent books might help others. They will trust you. Do not stop writing. It seems to be the vehicle for you to get messages out."

Smiling, He added, *You are good at it, but then you already know that.*

I will be honest, He said, *I had to laugh when you got so stuck on this writing retreat. You waited an entire year because of the pandemic when you could have done it virtually much sooner. Instead, you had the mindset that it had to be in person. I hope you have now realized to think on a greater scale and that sometimes things arrive differently than planned while accomplishing the same thing. Isn't it amazing? You would never sit down and do this on your own. You are too distracted all the time. Maybe,* He added with a laugh, *you need notes around you that say focus.*

One thing at a time. Trust the process, He reminded me.

"Yes, I know. I got the message!" I said as He continued to laugh at me. No matter how many times He joked, I was surprised every time. Whoever thought Jesus had a sense of humor!

"How do I shut out the outside noise? Life gets in the way."

He shook his head. *What about your Spirit Room? What about your beautiful backyard?*

"Why didn't I think of that?" I said as He laughed at me again. "I guess I felt that I needed to be in solitude to do this."

That is ridiculous. You need to exist on the planet. You need to live and have relationships with others. To connect with Me or your guides, all you have to do is push play, listen to your writing music, meditate, go within and ask for Me. It's quite easy. Don't make it so hard. It should start to become second nature.

I should have realized that, I thought, shaking my head.

"I am just blown away. I don't know how anyone will believe that these words are coming from You and aren't mine. Hmmm ... except You used some words that I would not typically say, so I am praying they will."

Fear not. As in all things, never fear. It is a complete waste of time, don't you think? He laughed again.

Do not get caught up in the process. Your mind is rambling again. Focus on the conversation. Focus on the story. Trust the process. Some will believe. Some will not. So what? Those you do reach will reach others, and so the process goes.

I will place opportunities for you to learn to open to your gifts. Pay attention to these messages or nudges. They will come from Me. I will guide you. Once again, dear one, trust the process. Share your story. The flock will come. Just finish this book.

"What else do you want me to know?" I asked.

Life is a process that will continue. People are evolving all the time. I hope that with this movement, they open and grow, practicing humility and kindness to others. Some will never understand until they come home how nasty and hurtful they have been. Those in power have egos, and they will never see it. They are stuck, and it is their life experience. I know you shun that behavior because of your gentle soul, and that is okay. I do not want you to see or know that. You see and feel things, and it disturbs you. I do not wish those elements to damage your Spirit. In this way, you can continue to do; I guess you would call it God's work. Shut out the noise, go within and be still. It serves you best and is the healthiest for you.

He added, *Just remember I am always here for you. Maybe soon I will be able to be present, and we can carry on a conversation. But even if you don't see Me, I know you feel My presence. I am here to help you. I just wish that more people would call on Me. Maybe after reading this, they will. That is My hope.*

"Is there anything else you want me to know? Is there anything you want to share?" I asked.

Just share your story and know that you are never alone, He said.

"Thank you. I now realize that. I am excited at the possibility of what awaits us all. Thank you for giving that clarity that I and so many others may need."

Remember when you saw the mist swirling around your girlfriend? That was an out-of-body experience. But Carol was highly evolved, and she left her body for a few minutes to see where she was going.

"I knew that had to be what happened. It was the most amazing thing I have ever witnessed! Initially I assumed my eyes were playing tricks on me!"

At the time I was a Realtor® and attending a continuing education class to maintain my license. My cell phone vibrated during the class and normally I would have let it go to voicemail, but I immediately recognized the number and stepped outside to take it. It was Carol's friend Diane, calling from Washington State to tell me Carol was in hospice and there may not be much time. I told her I would drive straight to the airport and get on the next available flight to Seattle. I prayed on the drive that there would be a standby seat available, and once on board my prayers continued during flight that I would make it in time.

Upon landing, I called Diane and was relieved to hear that Carol was still with us. Unprepared for the sudden trip, I was wearing a sleeveless spring dress and flip-flops – not suitable at all for Washington weather. Thankfully, my Mom's husband, Dick, met me at the airport with clothing, tennis shoes and socks, a toothbrush, toothpaste and a contact lens case. Lucky for me Mom and I were the same size! I quickly changed into the warmer clothes, then rented a vehicle and drove to see Carol.

Carol and I had met at the Seattle Times newspaper in 1973 and started our spiritual journey together in the mid-1980s. I was connected to her like no other. While Carol was drawn to diving deeper spiritually, at the time the old me was still growing and learning. "Debbie" was still stuck on why she was single and that was her main focus, because motherhood was the goal. Through the years, Carol had been taking numerous classes and learned healing processes through Training in Power™ (something I knew nothing about), and eventually became an instructor. Carol had evolved. She was an enlightened soul, therefore, the experience I would later witness made complete and total sense!

Arriving at the campus, I noticed all the beautiful flowers, lush lawn and green trees, a stark contrast from the dry Arizona desert where I now lived. Memorial cobblestones were in the garden as a memory to loved ones passed. The hospice building was separate from Evergreen Hospital, however, they are located on the same property in Kirkland. I felt a wave of peacefulness come over me as I approached the entry. The energy felt complete as I knew it was where Carol would eventually transition.

When I reached Carol's room, I was relieved to see she was alert and had her friends there. It was so good to hear her voice and see her smile. A couple of the ladies were students and another was also a teacher. It was a good night and I was grateful I had made it in time.

The next day Carol was sleeping. She rested all day, never opening her eyes. The day lingered on and late in the evening she started to fidget. With her eyes closed she would occasionally reach up and touch the oxygen tube. Everyone else had gone home hours earlier and it was just me and her other friend, Cat, in the room. I sat to Carol's right, while Cat was on her left. Carol was still fiddling with the oxygen hose so Cat asked if she wanted it off.

With eyes still closed, Carol nodded in agreement. Cat removed the oxygen hose and we both sat and watched Carol's breathing change. She was breathing long, deep and heavy and it seemed like forever between breaths. I tried to match her pattern but had to catch two to three breaths to her one. I was stunned at how she could go so long without air, when all of a sudden, on the part of her body that was exposed and not covered by a sheet, a mist started to appear swirling around her chest, just below her face. Thinking my eyes were playing tricks on me, as I had flown without my glasses and my contacts were in twenty-four-seven, I leaned in closer to make sure I was seeing correctly. I blinked a couple times in a feeble attempt to clear my contacts, then sat back.

Looking at Cat I asked, "Do you see *that*?"

She replied, "You see it *too*?"

We were both completely bewildered!

"Check the side of her bed," I said. "Look at the oxygen tube. Is it coming from there? Is there a leak somewhere?"

Cat checked, moving the nightstand, to find nothing. "No," she responded.

We both sat there without speaking and watched this mist, or vapor swirl around our friend's shoulders as she would only take a breath every sixty to ninety seconds. I had a hard time holding my breath for thirty! We were in awe of what was transpiring when just as quickly as the mist appeared it vanished, Carol started breathing normally and reached toward her nose, looking for the oxygen tube.

"Did you go somewhere?" Cat asked.

And, after over twenty-four hours of not speaking, Carol clearly and audibly said, "Yes," and smiled. Cat asked if she wanted the oxygen on again and she nodded her head in agreement.

I wish I had been able to speak to Carol. I would have loved to talk to her to find out what she saw. Seeing the mist was amazing and something I will never forget. If Cat hadn't been present to witness the mist, I would have thought it was my imagination as I was exhausted from traveling and emotionally drained.

In reflection I told Him, "It truly was a gift. My last one to receive from her, or so I thought."

Yes, it was the essence of her soul; however, notice how quickly it disappeared once she settled back in.

"It was magical, and I feel so blessed to have been able to witness that."

She knows that you speak of her.

"I can see her smiling now," I reflected.

I laughed as I remembered one particular post-it note on my desk. Carol had written on it, *Ask the Universe for it if you haven't already.*

"She knows it is there, I am sure."

Yes, she does. You can also talk to her, you know.

"Thank you. I find it hard because there is a part of me that wants to just be in one world or the other. How do I find balance?"

Do not worry. It will come to you naturally once you practice. First, start with meditation, so it is easier to connect. That will be the easiest step. Once you do that, it will happen naturally without effort. I will continue to get this message through to you.

"What? Is that message coming from *you*? Why didn't you say so? I would have done it then!"

He laughed, *Why does it matter who it is? The message is coming from a sacred space. We send different teachers hoping that one will resonate with each human and give them a gentle nudge. It is up to the person as to whether they act on it. For you, it is more challenging. You seem so strong-willed, and you allow procrastination to get the best of you at times. You need to be more FOCUSED and TRUST THE PROCESS. Those should be your new mantras. Whenever you see them remember that I am speaking to YOU.*

"Okay," I said, laughing. "Okay. I will. Thank you. It is all so overwhelming yet unbelievable."

I know, yet so it is, He said, smiling.

"I am so sorry my Spirit Room is in such disarray. It will not happen again," I promised.

I know.

"It should be one of my sacred places. It should be special. Thank you for instilling the inner belief I need in myself. I now know that I am capable. I know I can do this. I want to make the best use of my time and utilize it when I have the energy to do so. I promise. I will schedule a path. Thank You for showing me. Thank You for this awakening."

After you finish this book, I want you to dive right in and complete the other one. Remember your promise. Remember your commitment to Me. I do not want to see any more people waste their time being sad or unhappy. It goes back to what I said earlier today. It starts with the Golden Rule. It is so simple, yet here we go again.

However, before I go, I want to talk about something I mentioned earlier. It is about forgiveness. There seems to be so much hatred in your world today. I realize these are all lessons that presented themselves for people to learn but can you imagine hatred in heaven? No, neither can I. It does not exist, and somehow it needs to stop on your planet.

Forgiveness is so important to your well-being. When you forgive someone, it does not make what happened right or okay. However, when you forgive a person, you are letting go of that negative energy that will stifle your growth in this life, even if you never see the other person again. It will chip away at your soul and find a way to burrow deep inside you and block the essence of who you are. Then someone else comes along that either does something or wrongs you somehow, and you choose not to forgive them. That emotion nestles inside, finding a home alongside the other anger, and before you realize it, you have a mountain of ill thoughts built up deep inside you.

Think about it. Can you see this picture? Can you see how unhealthy it is? It will rob you of living your happiest and best life on the planet, so please find a way to let it go! That in no way means you must allow this person back into your life, but you can forgive them because they did not know any better, or possibly they did not care, but that is their cross to bear, not yours. Yes, it hurts. Yes, you are angry. I acknowledge those feelings but try sending them love. If you send love and send them on their way, it frees you up to attract love and goodness to you. I know some people have a hard time forgiving. Hopefully, they will read this and understand.

"Thank You."

Wow! And that was it. As quickly and quietly as He entered my space, He was gone. Now, in retrospect, saying thank you seems so trite, while almost feeling unreal. When I proofread what I wrote, I did not even remember writing! How can that be? I was not in my thinking brain. I was in my spiritual brain. Thank you, God. Thank You, Jesus.

What a gift.

Speaking of gifts, Carol had one more for me. In honor of her final wishes, her friends had obtained permission from the Washington State Ferry system and they set a date to stop at pre-set coordinates where they could release her ashes into Puget Sound. Unfortunately, I had to work at the airline and was unable to be there, so I asked her closest friend if she would have a long-stemmed pink rose to throw overboard for me along with theirs.

I received a text that the time was near so I went outside on my patio, turned the waterfall and soft music on, lit a tiki torch, and reclined on a chaise to meditate and pray. The evening was pleasantly warm and quiet. At seven thirty-five p.m. a gust of wind blew through my backyard and disappeared over my shoulders. It was the only breeze in the stillness of the evening. Later when Carol's friend contacted me, she told me they spread her ashes at seven-thirty, but I already suspected it. I knew the breeze was Carol coming through to let me know that she was finally free. Godspeed, my dear friend. Until we meet again.

CHAPTER TWENTY

TRUSTING THE PROCESS

Friday, August 20, 2021

We had planned on flying to Washington state to attend Stephanie's wedding, one of our daughter's sorority sisters, but my pulmonologist told me I could not travel. I had attended my niece's wedding in July in San Diego and caught what I thought was a cold. I have had pneumonia twice before; however, this time, I felt different. First, I was really sick, and then I lost my sense of taste and smell, plus the CT scan of my lungs showed ground glass nodules and there were opaque shadows. I attempted a thirty-minute drive to the cancer hospital for my monthly injection, but after thirty seconds in the car, I was afraid I would either cause a wreck or get in one, so I turned around and went home. Having driven a race car at Phoenix International Raceway, this was very unusual for me. I saw the stop sign, knew I was supposed to stop, but my reaction time was delayed! It made me very uneasy. My doctor said she believed I had Covid, even though I'd been fully vaccinated months prior. I was also too sick to drive and get re-tested. I was on steroids and other medications, and it took a while to return to a hundred percent. I was just praying that my lungs had cleared!

I cried that I couldn't attend this wedding. Steph is such a sweetheart and one of my *kids*. Even though I only have one child, I have many who call me Momma Ewing, and it fills my heart with joy. They know I would do anything for them. I love them all!

It also meant I wouldn't be able to visit my mother and her husband. She had turned ninety-two that Wednesday, which was during my writing seminar, so we had decided to celebrate afterward. I love my mom so much and was incredibly sad I couldn't go. I just wish things would turn back to normal!

In the meantime, the brutal Arizona summer had continued to drag on, with the temperature consistently above one hundred and fifteen degrees. It was a good time to complete projects inside, just as others do in the dead of winter in other states. Yes, it is hot, but we only have three months of unbearable weather, compared to rain, floods, or snow across the country that seem to go on forever. For me, living here is like heaven on earth.

I threw myself into deep cleaning mode and was pleasantly surprised to uncover twenty-four forgotten boxes of four-by-six pictures. My initial goal was to create photo albums, but can you imagine the space that would take up? Figuring there had to be a better way, I found a scanner online that could scan each picture in four seconds! What's more, Bill and I could sit on the couch and look at the photos digitally whenever we wanted, rather than having to retrieve them from the top shelf of a clothes closet. That became my project for the season, along with this book, of course, as I anxiously awaited this next writing retreat.

When the morning of the retreat finally arrived, I went into the office, turned on the music, lit my favorite candle, and created the ambiance necessary to get into the writing zone. When the office door is closed, my dear hubby knows not to enter. God bless him!

After a few exercises, the day begins. . .

Tom started with, "Trust me. Authors never die."

I repeatedly typed it like a mantra as Tom said it over and over, helping us to get into the zone.

"How do I feel?" Tom asked.

"I feel great!" Aww, yes, I know that He is with me.

"Authors never die. Authors never die. Trust me. Trust the process," Tom continued.

Then I hear *Him*.

Trust the process. Believe Me, dear, and it will unfold. Trust the process. Trust Me. Authors never die. Of course, you don't. Your book will go on after you have returned home, dear. That's why it is important to finish this book. There is a second one where you can help get through to so many who are suffering. You have a gift. I know you can help them. It is your journey. It is your passion. It is your purpose, as you know, dear one. I will show you the way. Trust Me, trust the process.

Surprised at just how easy this is, I asked, "Where are we going this weekend?"

I am not sure, but let's see what unfolds. The most important question is when will the book be finished?

"Yes. I'm supposed to be writing tonight. It has been a while. I am sorry. I am so sorry! I should have connected with You sooner."

All is well, my dear. It's in divine timing. It is all a process.

"I know. Even now, it's still hard for me to comprehend; however, I keep telling myself to *Trust the Process*. Do you see that I have sticky notes up?"

Yes, dear one. I do. Thank you. Is it working?

"Yes. For the most part. When I start to doubt, I see the notes and then laugh at myself. I just hope You will show me soon what steps to take to get the book published."

I will. You must listen. Listen for the messages. They are from Me, so don't ignore them or let your conscious mind enter into them. When you first hear it, trust the process. It is Me. Don't make it difficult for Me. Listen the first time, and things will all fall into place like those little black rectangular blocks with white dots, you know?

"Oh yes. Like dominos?"

Yes, they will start falling. You are still in the writing process, so be gentle with yourself. However, I want you to get organized. You know that is not one of your strong suits.

"Yes, of course, I know that!" I said, laughing. "I am taking another class to get and stay organized. I heard I need to clear space, so that is what I am doing. I am assuming others want to talk to me, maybe so I can help people? I don't know, but I am doing the clearing in my space and my energy field. I am learning Reiki. I am taking the steps I'm guided to take to see what unfolds, my energy permitting. Sometimes I feel like I move at such a glacial pace. After four years, I have finally settled into my new normal, but I will admit I am not fond of it. However, I am grateful that I am above ground and breathing and excited and anxious to see what unfolds. I don't worry much anymore about what other people may think. It doesn't matter. It is my truth. It is your truth. I just want to bring peace and comfort to others so they can live without fear."

Fear serves no one, dear Debra. It is a limitation that you place in your mind, and it grows and festers. It is not healthy. For whatever people fear, it usually never happens and is such a drain on one's energy. I do not know why people don't understand that. It is a waste of time, don't you see?

"Yes, of course, I do."

I want you to finish the book.

"I know. I know."

Please work on compiling it, and then we can see what we are missing, no? Start piecing it together. There are some stories you have left out. Every story has meaning. It will help to validate things.

"But people will think because it has been happening to me since I was young that it's something I was born with, and they will never be able to do it, never be able to listen and get messages."

Well, we need to find a way so they will believe. I know you think you are human. I know you think you are just a skeletal body with skin, but you are created in My image. You are divine. God is within you as He is everyone. Turn off the noise and clear out your space. Clear out what's running through your mind like a broken record player and truly listen. Quiet the mind and listen. That's what meditation is for. Why do more people not do this? I do not understand. We are all here. We are all here to help and guide, but nobody takes the time.

"Well, I have been guilty of that. I am still trying, however feeble, to do it daily. I signed up for a twenty-one-day meditation, and I have failed miserably. I only listened to three, and I am halfway done. What can You tell me so I can start my day with it? I truly want to, but I just think I have to get up, get to the gym and get my day going because I tend to run out of energy from this injection. I need to keep my breathing up, and the treadmill is the only way. By afternoon I fade. Maybe I could meditate in the afternoon when I am tired?"

Debra dear, I see you looking through your phone in the morning. You are reading emails. You are looking at social media.

I burst out laughing. "Of course, you see it all. Okay. Starting tomorrow, first thing I'll do when I wake up is listen to a meditation. I promise! I will start the habit! You caught me." I shook my head, "I guess I needed to have you call me out on my stuff. I am sorry. Now I am embarrassed."

It's okay, my dear. We all get caught up in life and get distracted. This month is a power month for you. You will see. Just wait. We have ten days left of the month. Remember I said this to you. I want you to reflect on it at the end of August. I know you will be smiling. It will all start to come together. Trust the process.

I start laughing again. "Ah yes, trust the process. I can't concern myself with the *How*. I just have to trust that You will lead me to the answer. Today I received the card in the mail. I sent one to that art company, You know? I was hoping they would help sponsor me with the publishing."

Yes, I am aware but do not be upset if you do not hear back. There are other opportunities.

"But You told me to give the book away for free."

Yes, I realize that because I want it read by thousands, but there will be those who want the paperback version. Listen to your publisher. She will guide you. She will help you with this. I have a good feeling about her.

"Wow. Thank you, so do I. We have a connection, and in my mind, have already chosen Shanda to do it for me."

So, get it done, my dear! Focus on your writing, even when you are not in a seminar. Why can you not commit to sitting down and spending the day with Me?

"Oh my God. I am sorry. When You put it that way, well, it makes me feel bad. Anyone would give anything to be able to connect with You this way. I apologize. I guess it's because You have been coming for so many years … I don't mean to appear as if I am taking our connection for granted. Now I feel ashamed."

No. Do not feel that way. We have only started talking. You weren't ready before, and I know it is still hard for you to believe that I can communicate with you this way. He laughed and added, *but I do.*

"I posted in this private group about something You said, along with the comment, 'Who knew Jesus had a sense of humor?' Someone responded, "I am glad you got to hear Him laugh." But I didn't hear You. I *saw* You, so I guess that means You visit others, and they have experienced this as well?"

Yes, my dear. You are not the only one.

"Okay. Hmmm…I thought I was special," I said laughing,

Well, You are. But everyone has something special about them.

"It also might help if those who have a relationship with You validated this as well. I know, even after reading the book they may still be afraid to share. I know it has taken me a long time to open up!"

Yes, possibly.

DAY THREE

Saturday, August 21, 2021

Eager for the day to begin, even though the prior two days were long and very emotional for me, I settled into my chair, recited the prayer and followed Tom's prompts.

"Smile. Hold that smile. Laugh. Giggle. Open up your heart. Chin to your chest… Eyes still closed… Nice deep breath in… Exhale deeply… Once more…ahhhhh."

Tom continues, "Eyes still closed, meet the presence of God in your mind… What does God have to say to me this morning? Good morning, God."

"What does God have to say to me today?"

"Hear with your heart…

Listen, listen, listen…

Breathe … breathe … breathe deeply….

What does God have to say to me this morning…?

What does Jesus have to say to me this morning…?

That's good. That's good. Listen to God. Listen with your heart.

Smile darn it. You're meant to be here you know. Laugh. Let me hear you laugh. Smile … Come on. It doesn't have to be work. Just in the flow, that's it…that's it. Don't be so serious. Welcome your co-author God. Smile! That's it.

Receive … receive … receive …"

I started telling myself, "Listen, Deb. He is here. What do You have to say to me this morning, Jesus? What do You have to say to me, God? What do You want me to receive today? What would You like me to hear today?" I continued as I started laughing as I felt Him draw near. "Okay. I can see You smiling. You are smiling because I actually meditated first thing."

Yes, dear one. I am proud of you. Please do that every morning. You will be amazed at how it assists you in living a better daily life. Not only will I be able to connect easier on a daily basis, but so will others. Keep at it, my dear. Keep at it. Let this also be a reminder to schedule things in your practice.

"Practice?"

Yes, you will see, but just be patient. There are building blocks that will be before you.

Listen, see, schedule, act.

Listen, see, schedule, act.

That will be your new mantra.

He paused. *There is still so much for you to learn, and you do not want to get behind. I know you want this book finished and ready by Christmas. While it is an admirable goal, dear one, you need to schedule it to accomplish that. Don't you understand by now that you need to schedule things to achieve them? You can't just – what do you say? – "fly by the seat of your pants"?*

I started laughing. "I haven't said that in years! Well, yes, You are right. I typically just wing it!"

My dear, there is too much sacred information waiting for you. No longer wing it. Please write it down, schedule it, check it off, and move on to the next. There is so much work for you to do before you come home. You are a lightworker. You are a healer. I will light the way, but it is up to you to follow it. Do you want to work with Me?

"Oh my God, oops, excuse me, of course, I do!!"

Then schedule it, dear one. Schedule it. We will go on a magical journey that is beyond your wildest dreams.

"I can feel it now as You say it. I imagine a magic carpet ride."

Well, if that helps you to visualize it, then so be it.

"But what about my life here? How will I be immersed in the spirit world and still have my life with my family and friends?"

Fear not. I will show you.

"So, do I schedule that too?" I asked, laughing.

He smiled and said, *You'll see. Trust the process.*

"You and that damn – er, sorry – trust the process again! Will I ever stop hearing that?"

Well, do you want to?

"No, I guess not."

Okay then, trust the process.

"I see. I see. Trusting the process is how I connect with You. I have not seen my guardian angels in years. Maybe I will see them again too?"

Yes, and possibly others.

"Last week, two angels came to me during a guided meditation. I was surprised as I have never seen angels before and have always wanted to. Sunny Dawn Johnston talks about angels all the time, yet I never experienced it until now. One had long blond hair and the other had long brown hair. Unfortunately, our time was brief. I will have to meditate again and try to bring them in. I would like to communicate with them. And, no," I said laughing, "They didn't have wings."

Take the steps. Go deep. Trust the process, and you will.

Deep in thought, I said, "I have a question for You.

Yes?

"Will I ever be able to connect with deceased loved ones as mediums do? I know I can see family members, but what about friends' loved ones, or even strangers for that matter?"

You have the ability. You are already halfway there, but your path is different. You can connect with loved ones if they are willing to connect with you.

"I want to see my grandma."

Don't you see her right now?

"Yes. Oh my God, yes! How did you do that?"

I didn't. You did. You can contact them at any time you would like. Just get into this state of consciousness and talk to them like you do me and see what they have to say. Do not be afraid. Debra dear, if you can connect with Me, why wouldn't you be able to connect with them? Think about that.

"Of course, of course. That was ridiculous, but I just never thought about it."

You will teach others to be able to do this.

"I will?"

Yes, of course, you will. You already know that. Aren't you going to have an automatic writing process to help the readers at the end of My book?

"*Your* book?" I asked, laughing.

Yes, My book. You are created in God's image. I brought you to this point. You are writing the book for Me, dear, to reach the masses. You are My vehicle. You are My lighthouse, don't you understand?

"Wow. Let me go deep with that. I thought it was my book." I said, shaking my head.

Well, it is your book, but you are writing My words. It is your story to draw people in so they feel comfortable and connect with you, but then that is where I come in. I do not want people to be afraid. I am so sad when I see what is happening on earth. I do not understand why there isn't more love. Don't they see that they all chose these experiences to learn?

"No, they don't," I said, "and some of them never will until they return time and time again."

Exactly, and that is what is unfortunate. Love is truly all there is. Love is the answer. I do not mean to sound cliché, but think of what a wonderful world this would be if everyone shared love. There is too much hatred, animosity, and anger, but then in My time we had it as well. Please read about Solomon. I know you don't know about the Bible. Excuse Me, you know about it but haven't read it. You do not know the story. Start with your daughter's book.

"Erica's children's bible?"

Yes, He said, smiling, *It has pictures. Remember? You like books with pictures.*

I started laughing then, because I have hundreds of books that I was drawn to when I bought them but never read.

"I also told my daughter that when I pass I want my books at my memorial for others to choose as keepsakes. Everything in my spiritual room is to be there, as gifts for my friends. The only thing that concerns me is if I live to ninety-eight or longer, I may not have a lot of my friends left."

Oh dear one, but you will have new ones! Unfortunately, your circle is small right now, but just wait. You will see it grow. Trust the process, He said, reassuring me with another smile.

I wanted to say, "Damn You" – jokingly, of course – but you can't say that to Jesus!

Oh, but I heard you! He said, laughing.

"Okay. I get it. You can hear and see everything, can't you!" I paused. "Sometimes I feel like I just want to hibernate and go within."

Then do that if you are called. It is an ideal way for you to shut off the outside world. You don't always have to connect with Me. You can just wait and listen for who or what comes through. I know you think you have to be in Sedona, but that is not necessary. You can go to Sedona in your room, exactly as you did with the therapist when you were in treatment for breast cancer.

"Thank you for coming through at that time."

I knew I needed to, dear. You were struggling. You forgot that I was here. I needed to remind you.

"I am so sorry I lost my way!"

Ah, but you didn't. They were all experiences you needed to go through to bring you to exactly where you are right now. Debra dear, you wanted to be a mother, so you did the work to be the best mom you could be. You are amazing. Don't you see how many people love you? I don't think you realize.

"I am just me."

And that, My dear, is the beauty in it. Many youths look up to you and listen. They know your caring ways and the love you have to give.

"Yes, but I lost a couple, and it hurt. I realize it was for their growth, but one I had known for years. They were my kids."

It was not their time. They have their path, and they need to be separate from you. So many times, ego gets in the way. They will find their way back if they are meant to. When this happens, you need to let go and let God take over, but always send them light and love. This will release the pain in your heart so you can be free to open up and love another, don't you see?

"Yes. Thank you. But it is tough when it is family."

Oh, My dear. You hang on way too tight. You should never hang on like that. They are not a possession, and besides, possessions are things, and you can't take them with you. So there is no need.

"Yes. I understood that over a conversation with my mother yesterday. I mentioned some things I would like to give away, and she asked me not to do it until she saw them. In my mind, I thought, *Mom, these are just things. You can't take them with you.* I am trying to release things that now appear as clutter. I don't want anything to hold me back from connecting with You."

Dear one, your mother is in her nineties. Just let her be. These things are important to her. They hold memories. She needs those memories at this stage of life. She needs to reflect on her life and all the good times she had, as there were many. Your mother is very fortunate to have a love of you and your brother and the love of two husbands.

"Yes, thank You for bringing Dick into our lives. He has been a Godsend."

Exactly, He said smiling, *Who do you think sent him?*

"Oh my God! I thought it was Judy, Dick's late wife, and my dad!"

No, dear. God sent him. God saw Judy and your dad. He didn't want either of them to miss embracing where they were with Me in heaven, so He had to ease their hearts, which was the best way possible. Your mother and Dick needed to be together. He knew they would be good together. He knew their lives would once again be joyful. He also knew your mother was older.

He smiled and said, *Why do you think He sent a younger man? So he would be there in her golden years to take care of her if need be. Caregiving is Dick's – do you mind if I call him Richard?*

"No, of course not!"

It is Richard's journey. He has a huge heart and a lot of love to give. He is living his purpose. Helping others is his passion, no?

"Yes, of course, it is. He has always been there for all of us!"

Exactly. Do you understand why God sent him now? Be patient with him, dear. I know sometimes you have a brush with him. Be patient as he ages. Remember these good times.

"Okay. Thank You." I started laughing, "He always talks about patience being a virtue, and it used to irritate the crap out of me because I didn't have any patience!"

Exactly, but you are getting better, aren't you?

"Yes. I am not completely there, but I am definitely getting better."

Meditate daily, and it will come.

"Wow, you get all these things from meditation?"

Yes. Why do you think people do it?

"To be honest, I didn't know. But, I mean, I can meditate and see pictures and then feel peaceful."

And then you also connected with Me in this manner. Meditation will open your eyes and heart to life, dear. Please make it a daily practice.

"Oh my gosh, I can tell you yes, but then if I fail I will feel guilty."

No, dear, don't ever feel guilty, but just keep trying. It will come with ease eventually, just like making the bed each morning.

"Okay, I will remember You said that. Thank you. Is there anything else You want me to know this morning?"

Well, do you have any questions, dear?

"Just a minute," I said as I continued some deep breathing exercises …

I can hear your thoughts. Take time for yourself. Schedule it, dear, and everything will be easy. It will eliminate stress in your life. It will be easier to stay on purpose, and you will reap the rewards. Remember that, dear one.

"But I want to know more."

Of course, you do. But, unfortunately, there is so much to learn that you will never be able to learn it all in this lifetime. So be patient with yourself. Read your daughter's Bible, meditate, and see what comes.

"Okay. I am at peace with that."

Good.

"Thank you. Thank you for talking with me this morning."

Oh dear, you do not have to wait for these writing sessions. Do you not understand that? You can connect with Me at any time. So why don't you?

"I don't know. I guess life gets in the way. I get distracted. I don't mean to put other things before You. That is never my intention. This was always my special time with You."

I know that. It is easy to slip back into life, and it is understandable. You receive no judgment from Me. But, remember, it is your journey. It's only yours and your decision what to do with it. It is all up to you. I can guide you; you can receive messages from others, but it is entirely up to you, dear Debra. It is your path for you to decide.

"But what if I take the wrong path?"

He laughed, shaking his head, *There is no wrong path. Don't you understand that?*

"Okay. I see. If I veer off on another path, then it's for me to learn and grow?"

Exactly, dear, don't worry about it. Trust the process.

Then He smiled and quietly left the room, and left me with a lot more to think about.

All is well.

Trust the process.

Listen, See, Schedule, Act.

I've got it!

Saturday Afternoon Session

After a much-needed break, Tom led us into another session. "Listen with your heart. What does God have to say to me today? What does God have to say to me today?"

Like a mantra on repeat, I heard, *Finish the book. Finish the book...* *See where you are today, and then we can reconnect. Trust the process. Be patient. Schedule it and act. Finish the book.*

"Okay," I said, relieved that He could come so easy.

Don't have any regrets, He reminded me.

Tom interrupted, "Breathe, exhale deeply, listen, write. Keep going. You can do this."

I assumed some couldn't connect as quickly as me, then I felt Him near again.

My dear, you are doing well. You are piecing everything together. I see you when you're in your Spirit Room looking at David's picture. He is aware that his picture is there. I know it is hard for his mother. I know it is hard for everyone who loves him. He is so sorry it happened. He didn't think it would, you know.

"Yes, I understand. They never think it will. I wish there weren't dangerous drugs that could hurt people. But, I guess we all have to decide what path we walk."

Yes. Each individual has their own journey. As parents, you can guide them. Sometimes they may veer off in another direction, either by peer pressure or curiosity. We can pray for them and do what is possible within our own power, but you must remember, whether someone reading this book believes it or not, it is a choice each individual makes when they are born. There are soul circles that congregate together, and some souls get together and decide to re-enter and re-experience life in a way to balance or neutralize things.

"Okay, so what I am hearing is that maybe I hurt someone in a previous life, so this time they hurt me to balance things out? If that is the case, I sure would like to know what I did!"

Yes, quite possibly.

"Well, why couldn't we just figure that out in heaven and apologize, hug and make up?"

Because you wouldn't learn what the lesson was trying to convey. You wouldn't feel how they felt. Do you understand?

"Sort of. It just seems like a lot of unnecessary pain to have to go through."

Not really. Think of it as a scene in a movie. You have to re-enact it to truly own and feel the experience so that wound can be completely healed and erased.

"Okay. That is interesting. I will have to learn more about that. While I may not like it, I guess it's a universal law, and we don't have a choice."

You always have a choice, My dear. It is something you decide together before you incarnate for your growth.

"Well, I don't like growing!" I yelled, laughing. "I feel as if I am talking to Kate now. I remember asking her one time, 'When did we ever stop learning?' Her reply was, 'Darling, you don't.' And I shouted the 'F' word at her, and I remember her roaring with laughter. When you think about it, we truly never do stop learning! I just wish some of the lessons were easier!"

Well, they can be, dear.

"How?"

Start each morning with meditation.

"There you go again! Talking about meditation!" I swear, I can't make this stuff up!

Well, it is because that makes everything possible. It helps to make your life flow. You can handle adversity much more calmly when it arises. Who wouldn't want that state of being?

"Okay. I guess I have more learning to do! I promise. I will meditate tomorrow morning."

My dear, don't do it for me, do it for yourself.

"Oh, I will, I will. If I make it a habit, or what does my friend Tajie call it? *Rituals and remedies.* Now that is interesting. Make it a ritual, and the outcome will be a remedy for the remainder of the day."

Ahh, He said, smiling. *Exactly. You understand.*

"I guess I know it is supposed to be good, everyone says it is, but I am the kind of person who needs to not only know the *why* but *feel the feeling.* Very interesting. Very insightful. I need to remember that."

Oh?

"Well, in January of last year, I signed up for this five-day vision board class by Colette Baron-Reid. I must tell you, it was an eye-opener and the best vision board class I have taken! I assume she teaches it every year, and I am looking forward to it again! I always thought vision boards were just cutting out pictures and pasting them down for you to see and hopefully manifest the things on the board. What I experienced was something different, and to be honest I don't even remember the steps, but I remember the *feeling.* My vision board is beautiful, and much to my surprise, some of the things are already coming true! I guess *feeling* and *believing* are part of the process toward manifestation, and I have to tell You, it's working!"

"As I am looking at it now, I see there are a couple of areas where I need work. So I'm getting a *message* to take screenshots, focus on just one area I want to manifest, and then move on to another. We are already eight months into the year, and I still have some things to do!"

Listen, see, schedule, act, He reminded me.

"I've got it!" I said, smiling.

Tom asked, "What does God have to say to you now?" He paused a beat, then repeated, "What does God have to say to you now?"

Jesus interjected, *You're doing good, my dear. Keep at it. You've got this, dear one.*

"Thank you!"

Tom ends the day with the prompt, "I am an author because … I am an author because …"

"I am an author because …" My fingers start typing faster, "… it is easier for You to connect with me in this way."

Yes, My dear, it is, and we had a great session today. I am grateful that you can connect with Me in this manner. I wish everyone would at least try. They would get answers to some of their problems if they just allowed it to happen. Maybe they will try it after they read our book.

"Oh, now it's *our* book?" I asked, laughing.

He smiles at me and says, *Yes, it is our book. We have done a great job. You are almost done.*

"We are almost done. Thank You for today. Thank You, Jesus, for today. I love You."

Well, I love you too, dear. Get some rest. We have a big day tomorrow.

DAY FOUR

Sunday, August 22, 2021

In preparation for class, I turned on my writing music and lit my favorite candle along with the faceted quartz crystal spire my daughter had given me. It sits on a lighted base which casts a pink hue across the room through the prisms. It is *my time* when I am in this zone, and I won't allow outside influences to penetrate it. It is sacred for me, and afterward takes me a while to come back to the reality of consciously living in the here and now.

That day, as I quietly waited, I heard the prayer recited to get us in a state of deeper consciousness. Tom came on and asked us to write:

"Why me, God?"

"Why me, God?"

I already knew where we were going. It is so easy for me to get there now.

Well, why not you? He said, laughing.

"Good morning, my friend. How are You today?"

The question, my dear, is how are you? I noticed you had trouble sleeping last night.

"Yes, I did. I couldn't shut my mind off. I kept trying to remember things and couldn't, so I sent myself a text. I didn't want to forget. Then, when I woke up in the morning, I tried to remember what it was and couldn't." I laughed. "So I am glad I wrote it down."

Yes, My dear, always do that. Once you clear your mind, it will be much easier for you to drift off to sleep.

"It's interesting that You say that. I felt it. I felt as if I were letting go."

I know you did. That was the point.

"This is so strange. I feel like I am just having a conversation with a friend."

Well, aren't you, My dear?

I laughed. "Yes, I guess You would say that. Of course You would." Then, changing the subject, I said, "I meditated this morning."

I know you did.

"I have two guides that I know have always been with me – Oonad and Anna, who I met during meditation in 1987. Anna was slender and beautiful. Initially, I was taken aback by Oonad as he was dressed in animal pelts that were jagged and uneven at the bottom. He was strong with broad shoulders, large hands and chiseled features. From the neck down he reminded me of a caveman, except his shoulder-length hair was tidy. Now someone new has come in. His name is Micah. I started to research the name because I felt he was from the Roman era. I had never seen him before. He was tall with chiseled features and brown chin-length straight hair. In retrospect, I also realized Anna was from my life when I had the dance studio."

Tom interrupts. "Ask God, should I keep on with writing? If so, why, and if not, why?"

I think you know the answer to that, My dear. Of course, you should keep on with writing, for that is how we connect; however, you are almost finished with this book. You need to read, have input, change, edit, and you will be done, dear.

"That is kind of scary for me."

Oh, but why?

"Because then I have to take the next step."

Oh, dear Debra, do not be afraid. Remember…

"Yes," I said, interrupting, "Trust the process!"

Of course! Always trust the process.

"I am getting much better at it."

I know you are.

You are also paying attention to messages. They will guide you to complete the publishing experience. Open the doors. There will be several. Did you not see one in an advertisement on television last night?

Laughing, I asked, "You were watching me?"

Always.

"Well, I turned it on an hour before bed. I just needed to decompress from yesterday."

I know. I know ... Yesterday was heavy for you. I could feel the weight of it all. That is why you could not sleep. You tossed and turned. Please listen to a meditation if you are struggling at night. Then you will just drift off to sleep.

"Okay. I thought about that. I will put earbuds on my nightstand so that it won't wake Bill."

Once again, Tom interrupts: this time with the question, "Am I getting in my own way, and if so, how will I clear it?

You are an open channel, My dear. He said that because he sees other participants struggling by their word count. You and I have got this. Fear not.

"Thank you. I know. Can I ask You a question?"

My dear, of course.

"Will I always have to write, or can You communicate with me in other ways? I mean, like when I am walking or laying down. Do You know what I mean?"

Of course, I do. Yes. Why don't you try it? You can talk to Me anytime, and I will come. However, you won't be able to document it like you do now.

"Oh. I like documenting things because when we communicate, I don't remember what we said until I read everything back."

You just explained an excellent example of something.

"What is that?" I asked.

When you are reborn, you have no memory of being in heaven, do you?

"No. There is no memory, and I wish there were."

Well, you come in as an infant, and you learn and grow. You have a certain imprint on a soul level of memories, I think you call them déjà vu? You know of what I speak?

"Yes, of course, I do! It's as if something happened before, or if I have been at a certain place before, though I have no memory of it."

Exactly. And that is what this is. When you were in Sedona and talked to your father, did you not experience the same thing?

"Yes! I had no idea of what I wrote! I was shocked that he told me to let go of the hammer."

And did he not tell you that all you had to do was think it over there, and you could have it?

"Yes, but I found it very hard to believe, let alone understand."

But then you read that in a book from a woman you respect and admire.

"Yes, and I jumped off the couch! There was no way that two people could say the same thing and never met! That validated what Dad had said. Not that I didn't believe my father, but come on, *All you have to do is think it over here, and you can have it? It sounded like a fairytale.*"

Reverend Janet Nohavec used to be a Roman Catholic nun. In 1996 she started The Journey Within Spiritualist Church in Lily Dale, New

York. Her friend Suzanne Giesemann co-authored her story in the book, *Through the Darkness*. In the book there was a comment about heaven and if there was something you felt you wanted, all you had to do was think of it and you would have it! I was so surprised to hear that not only from my dad, but also this respected minister and author!

Exactly. That is how heaven is.

"It's just so hard for me to imagine," I told Him.

Go deeper, my dear. Practice.

"Practice?" I was confused.

Yes, practice, so you can visit and see. Once you see more, you will understand, and then you can share your experiences and knowledge. The teachers will come. Meditate and listen for guidance.

"Okay, I will. Thank you."

Finish your studies, dear, but first finish editing this book. Get organized, clear things that are blocking you. I think you know what I mean.

"Yes, eliminate things in my home that no longer serve me. It has been a life-long habit, unfortunately, starting as a child. I remember cleaning my room and asking my mom what to do with the box of items. She always said to take it to the warehouse! The warehouse was in the back of our property of my childhood home where Dad's office was, including his building tools and our boat. So now the guest room has become my warehouse."

He starts laughing, *Yes, I know.*

"This has been such an emotional experience for me. It's still hard to believe that I am actually talking with You."

What? How can that be?

"Well, for God's sake, You are *Jesus!*"

I have always been here, dear. You just weren't ready. Now that you have taken the time, we will do this more. I want you to practice connecting when you aren't writing. Let's see how that goes, no?

"Yes, I would love that. Maybe I could even open an email and talk our conversation into it. Wait! I've done that before when I was floating in the pool!"

If that would make you feel better.

"I don't want to miss having our conversations logged. Oh! Speaking of conversations, the name of the book came to me last night."

Oh? What is that?

"You are smiling. You already know," I told Him.

Of course, I do.

"I don't want to use *Conversations with Jesus* because it would be like I stole that from *Conversations with God*."

But you are having a conversation with Me.

"Yes, I know that, but You have also visited me, and that is more important."

Is it?

"Yes! Of course, it is! I have *seen* You! Three times! The other times You've come have been in meditation."

Well, isn't that the same?

"No! My eyes are closed. The first, second, and third time, they were wide open."

Well, do you not see others, such as family and friends, during your meditations?

"Yes, but …"

Do not discount those experiences, dear. We visit in different ways. Do you not speak to them when you see them?

"Yes, of course, I do."

Then those are visits, My dear. Talk to them. Have a conversation with them such as we are now. It is the same. You can do it.

"Yes, but seeing You with my eyes wide open at the end of the bed was magical and magnificent!"

How would you feel if I did that now?

"It would initially shock me and probably scare the crap out of me!"

Exactly.

"Well, I could tell myself to breathe and look, and then hopefully, I would open my mouth! But, I mean, I stare at Your picture all the time."

I know you do. I am aware of that.

"It was the closest picture I could find of when You were standing on the rock in that meditation during the afterlife conference. It was distracting to me as the instructor kept counting down to have the participants go deeper, but it's as if I don't even need to count anymore. A couple deep breaths and I'm there! Still under, I had to leave my seat and move to the back away from the speaker. You and I went on our own journey that day while I blocked the teacher out. You popped in so easily! I wish I had documented all the times You have visited over the years. There is so much more I want to know."

Trust the process, My dear. Be patient. You will.

"Okay. I don't know how, but if You say I will, I will trust the process, study, and be patient. There is not really much else I want to do but learn more spiritually."

But do not get sidetracked. Remember, schedule it, believe it, and act upon it.

"Yes, I will. I will start that today. It will become another ritual."

I believe that is the only way you will master this, dear. After that, your life will go so much easier. Don't you have a feeling of accomplishment when you make your bed every morning?

I started laughing. "You can feel that? I will not start my morning until it's made."

Of course, I can. And don't you feel good about meditating the last three days?

"Yes, actually, I do."

I believe you are on track now for making that a habit, therefore today, I want you to get out your planner. Take thirty minutes after working on editing and schedule things for tomorrow. Trust Me, my dear, your life will go so much more smoothly, and it will eliminate stress. You will be able to handle the pressures of the day as they arise. Would that not be of a benefit?

"Oh my gosh, of course, it would!" Now I am embarrassed.

You run, as you say, helter-skelter, and that is not good. It would be best if you focused, but then you get distracted and are off in another direction. You believe you need someone watching over you. Didn't you feel that way when you worked at the newspaper?

"Yes, I did. I always felt that I worked better under pressure."

Pressure? Why would you do that to yourself, dear? That is not healthy!

"I know. I know. You're right. I want my life to flow with ease."

It is much better when you do. Focus, schedule, act, repeat. If you feel you need to answer to someone… He smiled *…then just know that I am watching.*

Laughing, I said, "Oh great! So, I have Jesus hovering over me!"

No, I do not hover, but you will know that I am there. I guide. Remember, I am always with you. I never left you, dear. I never left you.

"Thank you. Is there anything else I need to know right now for the book?"

I believe you have it under control, My dear. If anything is missing or you need to write about something more, I will let you know. Listen. Listen for Me. Listen for messages. Watch for signs. You will know it's Me. Go within, and I will tell you. Just please get the book done. Give away the book for free always, but you can list paperback books as well. Your publisher said to take pre-orders. That will help you financially to get My word out. Now I want to ask you a question...

"Okay," I replied, thinking, *Now* He *wants to ask* me *a question?*

Yesterday, I saw your frustration when you were writing, and your keyboard magically changed to a different language.

"Oh my God. Don't tell me. Was that You?"

He laughed. *Yes, of course it was. So you did not know that was possible?*

"No! How would I know that a Word document could be translated into a language other than English? I was so annoyed! I thought I would have to either reboot the computer or call my tech guy, but then I got up, left the office and came back in. Once I calmed down, I was open to receive the *message* to google it, thank God!" I laughed. "I don't remember the keystrokes but there was a way to change it back to English. At the time I was typing Russian and it happened twice! I just about snapped! And You think it was funny?"

That was a message, dear.

"A message? It was irritating!"

Do you not say everything happens for a reason…?

"Yes, of course," I said, wondering what He was getting at. "Oh! Oh! Oh my God! I get it! I get it! You want it in other languages!"

He smiled and said, *Remember the messages. Pay attention to the signs. They may be subtle, and other times they will be as plain as day. So pay attention, dear.*

"Okay, I will. I will."

Just get the book out. It is important.

"Yes, I understand. I cannot worry about what people will think. It is my story."

My dear, it is our story … It is our story, and I want to thank you for sharing it. I hope it brings comfort to the people. They should never be afraid. Once again, remind them to do the best they can, be kind to others, remember that there is a lesson in everything that happens, including the good and the bad, and most of all, spread love. You are all human beings. You are all the same. Please help people to see that.

"I will do my very best. Thank You."

Bless you, My dear.

And with that, He was gone.

IN CONCLUSION

As mentioned, by the time I get to the end of the sessions I have no memory of what has transpired. I know I had a conversation with Jesus, but I can only remember clearing space and scheduling things in preparation for the writing retreats, so it is always enlightening when I read it. One night, when I read what I had written during the previous day's retreat, I burst out laughing! Yes, it is hard for me to believe. Yes, it is hard for me to understand. And since I cannot explain what comes through my fingers onto the keyboard, I can only continue to trust the process because I feel and believe it is Jesus communicating with me. Whether you believe these writings or not, the choice is yours. It is my story. It is my relationship with Him, and it brings me overwhelming peace and comfort, not to mention an all-encompassing love I can't describe. My hope for you is that you will trust me. I have no reason to lie. I invite you to *trust your process*. What have you got to lose? And, if I start building an ark, I suggest you follow me!

At the back of the book is a link to my website, where you can receive an automatic writing process. I hope it will help you connect with a loved one, maybe even Jesus or the God of your understanding. I would love to hear about your experience, so please email me and let me know.

I am smiling as I write this because He dropped back in and is telling me to remind you that *love is the answer*.

Many blessings to you.

Much love,

Debra

ABOUT THE AUTHOR

Debra Moore Ewing is a spiritual intuitive, certified hypnotherapist, ordained minister, and past life regression practitioner.

Being in service to others is one of Debra's greatest passions. She has worked for a major airline for over twenty years, and is a proud third-generation Teamster and former union organizer who believes in equality for workers. She is also an eighteen-year breast cancer survivor and has been living with neuroendocrine cancer since 2017, and has worked tirelessly to support and educate others about these diseases.

Debra was a contributing author of *365 Days of Self Love,* published in October 2021. She is currently working on her second book, *Recovered, from a Person Who Loved Too Much.* Look for it in 2023. Jesus told her there's also third book, so she is excited to see what unfolds!

Born and raised in Seattle, she enjoyed a twenty-six-year newspaper career there before moving to Scottsdale, Arizona, where she lives with her husband Bill and their cat, Kosmo. They have one daughter, Erica, who is the light of their life, a son-in-law, Kyle O'Connor, who they adore, and their first grandchild is due in April.

REFERENCES

Afterlife Conference (www.AfterlifeConference.com)

Angelou, Maya quote retrieved from https://www.brainyquote.com/quotes/maya_angelou_383371

Baron-Reid, Colette (www.ColetteBaronReid.com)

Deustch, Stephen. (2006) *Conversations with God* [film]. CWG Productions LLC.; Cynthia R. Litman, Esq.; and Spiritual Cinema Circle.

Giesemann, Suzanne (2011) *Messages of Hope, The Metaphysical Memoir of a Most Unexpected Medium.* Missouri, Unity Books. www.SuzanneGiesemann.com

Harvard Health Publishing. (2012) "Steve Jobs' Cancer." https://www.health.harvard.edu/cancer/steve-jobss-cancer

Hay, Louise (1984) *You Can Heal Your Life,* Hay House Publishing.

Johnston, Sunny Dawn (www.SunnyDawnJohnston.com)

Karoub, Jeff. (2019). "Aretha Franklin's doctors recall her grace, grit." Retrieved from https://apnews.com/article/aretha-franklin-music-ap-top-news-mi-state-wire-detroit-bbc1f38e5c024c849669f268dd32b1e0

Look Good Feel Better, https://lookgoodfeelbetter.org/

Martin, Joel & Birnes, William J. (2017) *Edison vs. Tesla, The Battle Over Their Last Invention.* Skyhorse Publishing.

Mendez, Christopher, https://www.christopherpsychicmedium.com/

Miller, Robin (https://www.robinmillermusic.com/)

Nohavec, Janet (2011) *Through the Darkness, My Tumultuous Journey from Roman Catholic Nun to Psychic Medium.* Aventine Press. (www.JanetNohavec.com)

Perl, Sheri, *Helping Parents Heal; Electronic Voice Phenomenon.* (www.SheriPerl.com)

Pitstick Mark, MA, DC. (https://www.soulproof.com/)

Richardson, Kim (www.KimRichardson.Kim)

Schwartz, Dr. Gary. University of Arizona Advances in Consciousness & Health, Soul Phone, https://www.thesoulphonefoundation.org/meet-dr-gary-schwartz/

Shetty, Jay. 5-Day Habit Reset (www.JayShetty.me)

Southwest Institute of Healing Arts (www.SWIHA.edu)

Sutphen, Dick (1976) *You Were Born Again to Be Together.* Pocket Books.

Sutphen, Dick. (1980) *Master of Life Manual.* Valley of the Sun Publishing.

Sutphen, Dick. (1987) *Lighting the Light Within.* Valley of the Sun Publishing.

Tesla, Nikola quote retrieved from https://www.thesoulphonefoundation.org/soulphone-overview/

Tom Bird Writing Seminars (www.TomBird.com)

Training in Power (www.TrainingInPower.com)

Transcendent Publishing/Shanda Trofe (www.TranscendentPublishing.com)

University of Metaphysics (www.UniversityofMetaphysics.com)

IN CASE YOU'RE INTERESTED . . .

I highly recommend that you check the websites of the people I have referenced on the previous page. Many of them offer free classes that I think you will find interesting. One person in particular I would like to mention is Sunny Dawn Johnston. In 2020, at the height of the COVID-19 pandemic, she started a Facebook group, "Hearts Helping Humanity," which quickly grew to almost 7,000 strong and allowed her community to help others with food and other basic needs worldwide. She also started checking in with everyone live on her Facebook page, Monday through Friday, so we could all keep uplifted and connected while on lockdown instead of focusing on the constant barrage of bad and conflicting news we were seeing in the media. Always a genuine lighthouse for others, Sunny selflessly gave of her time to be there when her community needed it most. You can find this community at www. facebook.com/SunnyDawnJohnstonFanPage/.

And if you have ever thought of being an author, I highly recommend Tom Bird's incredible writing seminars. They will keep you focused and procrastination will become a thing of the past! You *will* write that book! You can check out his classes at: www.TomBird.com.

AUTOMATIC WRITING

I believe everyone can learn this process. Think about a hobby you have enjoyed. Were you good at it the first time? If you played sports, didn't you get better with practice? Of course, you did! Every time you practiced, you got better! It's the same with automatic writing. Practice, believe, trust the process, and it will happen. If you feel like sharing, I'd love to hear about it! You can access the Automatic Writing instructions on my website:

www.DebraMooreEwing.com